D1511629

BASIC / NOT BORING
MATH SKILLS

WHOLE NUMBERS & INTEGERS

Grades 6–8⁺

Inventive Exercises to Sharpen
Skills and Raise Achievement

Series Concept & Development
by Imogene Forte & Marjorie Frank
Exercises by Terri Breeden & Andrea Sukow

Incentive Publications, Inc.
Nashville, Tennessee

About the cover:
Bound resist, or tie dye, is the most ancient known method of fabric surface design. The brilliance of the basic tie dye design on this cover reflects the possibilities that emerge from the mastery of basic skills.

Illustrated by Kathleen Bullock
Cover art by Mary Patricia Deprez, dba Tye Dye Mary®
Cover design by Marta Drayton, Joe Shibley, and W. Paul Nance
Edited by Anna Quinn

ISBN 0-86530-369-X

PRINTED IN THE UNITED STATES OF AMERICA

TABLE OF CONTENTS

CELEBRATE BASIC MATH SKILLS

Basic does not mean boring! There certainly is nothing dull about plunging into the world of sports and using your skills with numbers to . . .

 . . . figure out who gets paid what salary in the world of sports

 . . . sort out fascinating trivia about athletes and sporting events

 . . . score a bowling contest or a golf game between past U.S. presidents

 . . . unravel mystery quotes and names of athletes

 . . . tell the Wildcats from the Bobcats from the Cougars and other feline mascots

 . . . solve problems to find nicknames of famous athletes or prices of courtside seats

 . . . decide whether a racing pigeon moves faster than a guy on a skateboard

 . . . help you translate an Olympic motto from Latin

 . . . decide whether a whale can jump farther than a human

The idea of celebrating the basics is just what it sounds like—enjoying and improving the basic skills of solving math problems. The pages that follow are full of exercises for students that will help to review and strengthen specific, basic math skills. This is not just another "fill-in-the-blanks" way to learn. The high-interest activities will put students to work applying a rich variety of the most important skills and facts related to whole numbers and integers. And kids will do this good work while enjoying fun and challenging adventures with fascinating sports information, statistics, and personalities.

The pages in this book can be used in many ways:
- for individual students to sharpen a particular skill
- with a small group needing to relearn or strengthen a skill
- as an instructional tool for teaching a skill to any size group
- by students working on their own
- by students working under the direction of an adult

Each page may be used to introduce a new skill, to reinforce a skill, or to assess a student's performance of a skill. As students take on the challenges of these adventures with problems, they will grow in their mastery of basic skills and have a good time while they do it. And as you watch them check off the basic math skills they've strengthened, you can celebrate with them!

-7^2

$1,312$

$-3 \times -5 = 15$

55

-12^3

$8^3 =$

$+$

114^2

$25,379$

37

SKILLS CHECKLIST FOR WHOLE NUMBERS & INTEGERS

✔	SKILL	PAGE(S)
	Read and write whole numbers	10
	Identify place value of whole numbers	11
	Write whole numbers in expanded form	12
	Compare and order whole numbers	13
	Round whole numbers	14
	Add and subtract whole numbers	15–17
	Identify and use properties of operations	18
	Identify and use properties of numbers	19
	Identify and understand multiples of numbers	20, 21
	Find common multiples and least common multiples	21
	Multiply whole numbers	22–24
	Divide whole numbers	25, 26
	Understand divisibility and identify factors	27
	Identify prime and composite factors	28
	Read and write numbers with exponents	29
	Read, write, and use numbers which are powers of ten	30–32
	Multiply by powers of ten	31
	Divide by powers of ten	32
	Solve word problems with whole numbers	33–35
	Estimate answers to whole number operations	36, 37
	Solve equations with whole numbers	38, 39
	Select the proper operation for a given computation	40
	Read, write, compare, and order integers	41–43
	Place integers on a number line	42, 43
	Add and subtract integers	44
	Multiply integers	45, 46
	Divide integers	47
	Solve equations with integers	48, 49
	Graphing integers on a coordinate plane	50

WHOLE NUMBERS & INTEGERS

Skills Exercises

$$1,000,000$$

$$X = -10 \div$$

$$-3 \; X \; -5 = 15$$

YOU NEED A BIG CITY

Professional baseball is a big-city game. Only a large metropolitan area can provide enough money and fans to support a team. Complete the following exercises that describe some major league cities.

I. Write in words the population of these National League Baseball locales.

Team Name	Population	
1. Chicago Cubs	2,783,726	_____
2. New York Mets	7,322,564	_____
3. Philadelphia Phillies	1,585,587	_____

II. Write the population of these National League Baseball locales in standard form.

Team Name	Population	
4. Atlanta Braves	Two million, eight hundred thirty-three thousand, five hundred eleven	_____
5. Cincinnati Reds	One million, seven hundred forty-four thousand, one hundred twenty-four	_____
6. Houston Astros	Three million, seven hundred eleven thousand, forty-three	_____
7. Los Angeles Dodgers	Eight million, eight hundred sixty-three thousand, one hundred sixty-four	_____

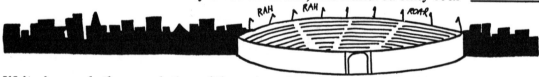

III. Write in words the population of these American League Baseball locales.

Team Name	Population	
8. Baltimore Orioles	2,382,172	_____
9. Cleveland Indians	1,831,122	_____
10. Detroit Tigers	4,382,297	_____
11. Milwaukee Brewers	1,607,183	_____

IV. Write the population of these American League Baseball locales in standard form.

Team Name	Population	
12. Kansas City Royals	One million, five hundred sixty-six thousand, two hundred eighty	_____
13. Oakland Athletics	Three hundred seventy-two thousand, two hundred forty-two	_____
14. Seattle Mariners	One million, nine hundred seventy-two thousand, nine hundred sixty-one	_____

Name _____

BIG MONEY FOR BIG ATHLETES

You've heard about multimillion dollar contracts for athletes, haven't you? Read about these big salaries in professional sports while you practice your knowledge of place value.

1. In 1995, Chris Miller of the St. Louis Rams was forced to give up the game and his nine million dollars in salary. He had suffered his sixth concussion in fourteen months. Write his salary in standard form.

   _____

2. The professional basketball player Juwan Howard was pursued by several teams. The Bullets were able to get him to join their team with a $105,000,000 offer. What is the value of the 5 in his salary?

   _____

3. Tiger Woods is the man to watch in professional golf. In one year he received $60,000,000 in sports endorsement contracts. What place value position does the 6 hold in this large number?

   _____

4. Alex Rodriguez, an American League MVP, negotiated a new contract with the Seattle Mariners. He signed a three-year extension for $10,250,000. What place value position does the 5 hold?

   _____

5. Mark Brooks, a professional golfer, made $1,430,000 in one year. What is the value of the 4 in his earnings?

   _____

6. Mike Tyson, heavyweight boxer, beat Bruce Sheldon in a 109-second fight. Mike Tyson earned $137,615 per second. What is the value of the 6 in his earnings?

   _____

7. The Lakers' contract with Shaquille O'Neal is worth $120 million. What is the value of the 1 in O'Neal's contract?

   _____

8. Michael Jordan received the richest one-year contract in the history of sports. He was paid $25,000,000 for a one-year deal. What digit is in the ten millions place in this figure?

   _____

9. In a very unfriendly game between the Oilers and the Steelers, the teams' fines totaled $145,000. What is the place value of the 1 in this large number?

   _____

10. Jarome Iginla, a professional hockey player, signed a three-year contract worth $850,000. What is the value of the 8 in this number?

    _____

Name _____

FANS LOVE STATS

Sports are filled with interesting statistics (they're called stats). Read the stats below and then write the given number in expanded form.

1. Dave "Tiger" Williams piled up 3,966 penalty minutes in hockey. Write 3,966 in expanded form.

_____

2. In 1945 the penalty for punching an umpire was lifetime banishment from baseball. Write 1945 in expanded from.

_____

3. When Team USA defeated Canada in the hockey World Cup only 767,200 U.S. households watched the game. Write 767,200 in expanded form.

_____

4. Did you know that there are 162 games in a full season of baseball? Write 162 in expanded form.

_____

5. In 1996 there were 4,962 home runs hit. Write 4,962 in expanded form.

_____

6. When Kirby Puckett announced his retirement from baseball, he stood before 51,011 fans. Write 51,011 in expanded form.

_____

7. Ohio State University has a great football team. In only six games into the 1996 season their total offensive output was 2,962 yards. Write 2,962 in expanded form.

_____

8. Frank Eliscu was the sculptor of the Heisman Trophy. He died in 1996 at the age of 83. Determine the year of his birth, and write it in expanded form.

_____

9. When the famous racehorse, Cigar, won the Arlington Race, over $200,000,000 worth of tickets went uncashed. The memento of the ticket was worth more than the payoff. Write 200,000,000 in expanded form.

_____

10. In 1996, the Celtics basketball team took 6,942 shots. Write 6,942 in expanded form.

_____

11. Courtside seats at the Los Angeles Lakers game cost $600 each. This price includes a program and waiter service. Determine how much it would cost to attend six games. Write this answer in expanded form.

_____

12. Jason Kidd became the sixth player in NBA history to register 783 assists and 553 rebounds. Total these two numbers and write your answer in expanded form.

_____

Name _____

BIG BUCKS FOR GOOD SEATS

If you've never tried to buy tickets to an NBA (National Basketball Association) game, you may be shocked at these ticket prices. But this is the kind of money you'll need to have, if you want to get up close to the action and sit at courtside!

COURTSIDE SEAT PRICES:

CHARLOTTE HORNETS $180.– 100276534

CHICAGO BULLS $400. ZN103

COURTSIDE $375.⁰⁰ HOUSTON ROCKETS

LOS ANGELES CLIPPERS $275.⁰⁰

MINNESOTA TIMBERWOLVES COURTSIDE $174.

COURTSIDE TICKET L.A. LAKERS $600.–

N.Y. KNICKS $1000.⁰⁰

1. List the team and the ticket prices from most expensive to least expensive.

Team	Ticket Price

2. Which would cost more, three tickets to a Chicago Bulls game or five tickets to a Charlotte Hornets game? How much more? _____

3. Which would cost more, two tickets to see the Los Angeles Lakers or five tickets to a Chicago Bulls game? How much more?_____

4. Which would cost more, three tickets to a Los Angeles Clippers game or four tickets to a Charlotte Hornets game? How much more? _____

5. Which would cost more, five tickets to a Houston Rockets game or two tickets to a Los Angeles Lakers game? _____

6. Mrs. Martinez's class of 25 students wants to go to see a professional team play. If they raise $10,000 for tickets, which teams could they see for one game? _____

7. William won $5,000 in a radio sports contest. The money had to be spent on tickets. He has four good friends that he wants to take to the game with him. On the back of this page, write a possible budget to spend his winnings. (Don't forget to include William's tickets.)

Name

BALLPARK FIGURES

The expression "ballpark figure" means an estimate or a round number. For instance, you might ask your mom to give you a ballpark figure for how much she's planning to spend on your birthday present. Follow the directions to get a ballpark figure for each number below.

WOW! IT'S OUTTA THE BALL PARK !

SLAM

I. Round to the nearest ten.

1. 534 _____   6. 43 _____
2. 793 _____   7. 9 _____
3. 1,247 _____   8. 58 _____
4. 6,872 _____   9. 573 _____
5. 795 _____   10. 2,265 _____

II. Round to the nearest hundred.

11. 582 _____   16. 360 _____
12. 1,234 _____   17. 575 _____
13. 640 _____   18. 3,987 _____
14. 770 _____   19. 4,231 _____
15. 1,104 _____   20. 929 _____

III. Round to the nearest thousand.

21. 3,109 _____   26. 4,765 _____
22. 2,786 _____   27. 7,954 _____
23. 4,876 _____   28. 54,876 _____
24. 8,543 _____   29. 543,908 _____
25. 2,264 _____   30. 6,832 _____

IV. Round to the nearest ten thousand.

31. 41,876 _____   36. 789,555 _____
32. 260,098 _____   37. 86,452 _____
33. 91,975 _____   38. 755,555 _____
34. 207,865 _____   39. 7,643 _____
35. 462,876 _____   40. 54,321 _____

Name _____

FEARSOME FELINES

Not all cats are the kind you want to curl up with by the fire. Many cats are college and professional sports teams fighting out competitive battles on the fields or courts. Solve the problems to get a number code for each letter below. Then use the codes to find the "cat" names of the teams described below.

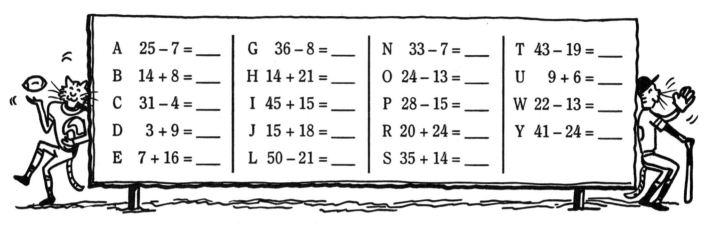

A 25 − 7 = ___	G 36 − 8 = ___	N 33 − 7 = ___	T 43 − 19 = ___
B 14 + 8 = ___	H 14 + 21 = ___	O 24 − 13 = ___	U 9 + 6 = ___
C 31 − 4 = ___	I 45 + 15 = ___	P 28 − 15 = ___	W 22 − 13 = ___
D 3 + 9 = ___	J 15 + 18 = ___	R 20 + 24 = ___	Y 41 − 24 = ___
E 7 + 16 = ___	L 50 − 21 = ___	S 35 + 14 = ___	

___ ___ ___ ___ ___ ___ ___ ___
9 60 29 12 27 18 24 49

1. Mascot name shared by Villanova, University of Arizona, Kansas State, and Northwestern University

___ ___ ___ ___ ___ ___ ___
22 23 26 28 18 29 49

2. Cincinnati's pro football team

___ ___ ___ ___ ___
29 60 11 26 49

3. Penn State's famed Nittany _____ ; Detroit's pro football team

___ ___ ___ ___ ___ ___ ___ ___
13 18 26 24 35 23 44 49

4. Carolina's pro football team and University of Pittsburgh's mascot

___ ___ ___ ___ ___ ___
24 60 28 23 44 49

5. Detroit's pro baseball team; mascot of Tennessee State, Princeton, and Louisiana State (although these are "fighting")

___ ___ ___ ___ ___ ___ ___
22 11 22 27 18 24 49

6. University of Ohio and Southwest Texas State mascot

___ ___ ___ ___ ___ ___ ___
27 11 15 28 18 44 49

7. Washington State and University of Houston mascot

___ ___ ___ ___ ___ ___ ___
33 18 28 15 18 44 49

8. Southern Baton-Rouge University mascot

Name

STRIKES, SPARES, & SCORES

Brianna, Mark, Jana, and Jay have decided to spend the afternoon bowling. While some lanes have computers that keep score for the bowlers, the four friends have chosen to go to the lanes where the competitors get to keep their own score. Each bowler's turn involves trying to knock down all ten pins with at most two balls. Each player's turn is scored in one frame.

EXAMPLE:

On her first turn, Jana knocked down all ten pins with one ball. That's a STRIKE (scored with an X). On her next turn she knocked down five pins with the first ball and three pins with the second. To calculate her score for the first frame she gets to add the ten points from her strike to the total pins for her next two balls (10 + 5 + 3 = 18).
So her score after frame one is 18. To get her score for frame two she adds her previous score to the total pins knocked down by her next two balls (18 + 5 + 3 = 26), so her score after two frames is 26.

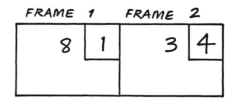

FRAME 1   FRAME 2

X | 5 | 3
18 | 26

 1. In the first frame Brianna knocked down eight pins with her first ball and one pin with her second ball. In the second frame she knocked down three pins with the first ball and four pins with the second ball. Calculate her score in each of the first two frames.

FRAME 1   FRAME 2

8 | 1   3 | 4

 2. Mark rolled a gutter ball on his first throw and knocked down all ten pins with his second ball—that's a SPARE (scored with a /). In the second frame, he knocked down six and two with his two rolls.

    a. To score the first frame, add ten pins from his spare to his first ball (six pins) from the second frame.

    b. To score the second frame, add his score from part (a) to the pins from his two rolls in the second frame.

FRAME 1   FRAME 2

– | /   6 | 2

Use with page 17.

Name

STRIKES, SPARES, & SCORES, CONTINUED

Use with page 16.

 3. Jay knocked down two pins on his first roll and knocked down the other eight with his second ball (that's a _____). In the second frame, he knocked down nine pins with his first ball and zero with his second. Calculate his score for these two frames.

FRAME 1	FRAME 2
2 ⟋	9 –

 4. After the first game the players decide to compare scores.

Player's names	After 5 frames	Final scores
Brianna	59	118
Mark	84	135
Jana	72	124
Jay	68	136

a. What was the difference in Brianna and Jana's score after five frames? _____

b. By how many pins did Mark's final score exceed Brianna's? _____

c. If Brianna and Mark were partners, how much did the sum of their scores lead Jana and Jay's after five frames? _____

d. By the end of the first game Jana and Jay were the winners. By how many pins did they win? _____

 5. Below are the first five frames for the second game played by the four friends. Total up their scores for each of the frames.

1.

| 4 2 | – 9 | ⊠ | 6 ⟋ | 8 1 | Sylvia: |

2.

| 3 5 | 7 ⟋ | 7 – | 5 ⟋ | 6 2 | Mark: |

3.

| – 8 | 4 ⟋ | ⊠ | 1 7 | 3 5 | Jana: |

4.

| ⊠ | 9 – | 2 ⟋ | 8 1 | 6 3 | Jay: |

Name _____

KNOWING THE GAME PLAN

In football, the coach can call many different plays. Each player needs to know what the plays are, or all the plans and rules won't do much good. Each play requires each player to know how, when, and where to perform his assigned tasks. In math, the properties of operations are kind of like football plays. They tell each player (number) what tasks they can do. You'll need to use three properties of operations: **commutative, associative,** and **distributive,** to solve these problems.

1. Mark thinks of the commutative property as the order of his daily travels from home to school and then from school to home. Fill in the missing numbers to complete the following examples of the commutative property.

   (a) $7 + 3 = \_\_\_ + 7$ (b) $5 \times \_\_\_ = 8 \times 5$

2. Tonya considers the grouping of the associative property to be like driving to pick up her two best friends. Sometimes she picks up Jessica first and then Mary, and other times she picks up Mary first and then Jessica. Either way, all three friends get to their activities. Complete the following equations using the associative property.

   (a) $(2 \times 5) \times 7 = 2 \times (5 \times \_\_\_)$ (b) $(3 + \_\_\_) + 8 = 3 + (7 + 8)$

3. If the order of the numbers is what changes, think *commutative*. If the grouping of the numbers changes, think *associative*. Identify the following as commutative (**C**) or associative (**A**) property examples.

   (a) $2 + (4 + 9) = 2 + (9 + 4)$ _____   (d) $(7 + 4) + 3 = 7 + (4 + 3)$ _____

   (b) $(3 \times 5) \times 10 = 3 \times (5 \times 10)$ _____   (e) $2 \times (8 \times 9) = (8 \times 9) \times 2$ _____

   (c) $(1 + 6) + 8 = 8 + (1 + 6)$ _____   (f) $(8 \times 6) \times 5 = 8 \times (6 \times 5)$ _____

4. Complete the following examples using the distributive property.

   (a) $7(3+1) = \_\_\_ \times 3 + \_\_\_ \times 1$ (b) $5 \times 8 + 5 \times 2 = \_\_\_ (8+2)$

5. Rearrange the following equations using the given property.

   a) associative $12 + (7 + 3) =$ _____   b) associative $6 \times (8 \times 2) =$ _____

   c) commutative $(5 + 11) + 9 =$ _____   d) distributive $10 (4 + 3) =$ _____

   e) distributive $6 \times 5 + 6 \times 2 =$ _____   f) associative $1 + (9 + 5) =$ _____

   g) commutative $12 \times (4 \times 7) =$ _____   h) commutative $(2 \times 7) \times 11 =$ _____

   i) associative $(8 \times 10) \times 2 =$ _____   j) commutative $(3 + 8) + 14 =$ _____

Name

THE RULES OF THE GAME

All sports have rules. Whether it's an individual sport such as golf, tennis, or speed skating, or a team sport such as baseball or volleyball, participants get into trouble if they don't know and follow the rules of the game. In math, the properties of numbers are a lot like game rules. Properties tell you what numbers can and cannot do as a part of the game plan. Here are some of the properties that you need to know well in order to correctly solve math equations.

Identity Property	**Property of Zero**	**Inverse Property**
$5 + 0 = 5$	$6 \times 0 = 0$	**of One**
$7 \times 1 = 7$		$2 \times (\frac{1}{2}) = 1$

1. Complete the following equations using identity, inverse, and zero properties.

   (a) ___ $+ 3 = 3$ (c) ___ $\times 8 = 0$ (e) $(\frac{1}{4}) \times$ ___ $= 1$

   (b) $0 +$ ___ $= 2$ (d) $5 \times$ ___ $= 1$ (f) $1 \times$ ___ $= 9$

2. Identify whether the following are examples of the identity, inverse, or zero properties.

   (a) $(\frac{2}{3}) \times (\frac{3}{2}) = 1$ (d) $0 + 4 = 0$ (g) $0 = 6 \times 0$

   _____   _____   _____

   (b) $12 \times 0 = 0$ (e) $2 = 2 \times 1$ (h) $1 = 7 \times 1$

   _____   _____   _____

   (c) $11 \times 1 = 11$ (f) $1 = (\frac{1}{5}) \times 5$ (i) $2 = 0 + 2$

   _____   _____   _____

3. Select the letter below that correctly identifies what property the equations illustrate.
   A. Identity   C. Zero Property   E. Commutative
   B. Inverse   D. Distributive   F. Associative

   _____ 1. $5 + 1 = 1 + 5$ _____ 5. $(3 + 9) + 10 = 3 + (9 + 10)$

   _____ 2. $0 = 0 \times 7$ _____ 6. $(2 \times 5) \times 8 = 8 \times (2 \times 5)$

   _____ 3. $2 \times 3 + 2 \times 7 = 2 (3+7)$ _____ 7. $(4 + 9) = (4 + 9) + 0$

   _____ 4. $6 \times (\frac{1}{6}) = 1$ _____ 8. $1 \times (11 \times 6) = (11 \times 6)$

Name _____

SPORTING MULTIPLES

Athletes love multiples—as long as you're talking about multiple scores or points, and not injuries! Use your knowledge of multiples to solve these problems.

1. Too Tall Tom is great at three-pointers in basketball. Write the first ten multiples of 3.

_____

2. The Big Bruisers are great at touchdowns. Write the first ten multiples of 6.

_____

3. The Much-Muscle Football Team always makes the extra point each time they score a touchdown. Write the first ten multiples of 7.

_____

4. Each time Sugar Foot Steve shoots the basketball from the left side of the court, he scores 2 points. Write the first ten multiples of 2.

_____

5. Fill in the scoreboards for these games.

a. Cougars: 4 touchdowns (6 pts each); 3 extra points (1 pt each); 3 field goals (3 pts each)
   Panthers: 5 touchdowns (6 pts each); 1 extra point (1 pt each); 1 field goal (3 pts each)

SCORE	
COUGARS	
PANTHERS	

b. Bobcats: 29 goals (2 pts each); 6 three-point goals (3 pts each); 18 free throws (1 pt each)
   Wildcats: 35 goals (2 pts each); 5 three-point goals (3 pts each); 5 free throws (1 pt each)

SCORE	
BOBCATS	
WILDCATS	

c. Lions: 9 innings; 4 runs in each inning
   Tigers: 9 innings; 3 runs in each of four innings; 5 runs in each of the other innings

SCORE	
LIONS	
TIGERS	

d. Cougars: 44 goals (2 pts each); 22 free throws (1 pt each)
   Jaguars: 39 goals (2 pts each); 19 free throws (1 pt each)

SCORE	
COUGARS	
JAGUARS	

Name _____

20

CMs & LCMs

How are you with your CMs and your LCMs? Do you remember what these are?

A **common multiple** is a multiple that 2 or more numbers have in common.
Ex: 12 is a **common multiple** for 2, 3, 4, and 6.

A **least common multiple** is the smallest number that is a common multiple for 2 or more numbers.
Ex: 4, 8, 12, and 16 are **common multiples** for 2 and 4, but 4 is the **least common multiple.**

1. The Wildcats Football Team made the extra point after every touchdown for 7 points each time they scored. The Cougars made only the touchdown each time they scored, for 6 points each time. What is the lowest score at which the game would be tied? _____

2. The Hit-A-Homer Baseball Company ships their baseballs in cases of 6. The Super Slugger Baseball Company ships their baseballs in cases of 8. What is the fewest baseballs you would have to order to get the same number of balls from each company in full cases? _____

3. Molly Muscle is putting weights on her machine. Each of her weights are 5 pounds. Pump-It-Up Polly wants to have the same amount of weight on her machine as Molly, but her weights are 12 pounds each. What is the least amount of weight that could be placed on both machines so that the women are lifting the same amount? _____

4. The Burros have scored only 2-pointers in the basketball game and the Tornadoes have scored only 3-pointers in the game. Is it possible for the score to be tied at 18 to 18? _____

Write 5 common multiples for each of these sets of numbers:

5. 4, 5 ____ ____ ____   6. 2, 5, 6 ____ ____ ____   7. 3, 7 ____ ____ ____

8. 6, 4 ____ ____ ____   9. 3, 15 ____ ____ ____   10. 2, 16 ____ ____ ____

Find the least common multiples for the following numbers:

11. 14, 22 _____   12. 12, 20 _____

13. 9, 15 _____   14. 12, 25 _____

15. 10, 15 _____   16. 4, 7, 9 _____

17. 3, 5, 12 _____   18. 6, 16, 26 _____

19. 150, 375 _____

Name _____

CYCLE THE DISTANCE

Tom, Jane, and Jonathan ride their bicycles on the paths around town, each riding several miles a day. Below is a map of the points around town. Also listed are the distances between points on the map. Draw lines between points that are connected, and write in the distance in miles between the points on the map. Help our cyclists to compute the distances and times for their bike rides to answer the questions on the next page (page 23).

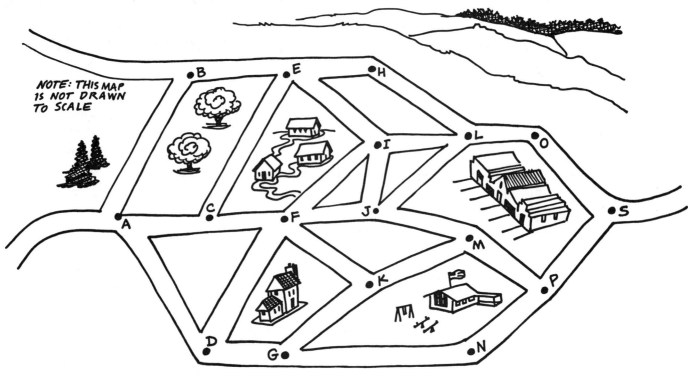

From	To	Distance	From	To	Distance	From	To	Distance
A	B	3 miles	E	I	4 miles	J	L	4 miles
A	C	1 mile	F	I	6 miles	J	M	4 miles
A	D	2 miles	F	J	5 miles	K	M	3 miles
B	E	2 miles	F	K	4 miles	L	O	6 miles
C	E	4 miles	G	K	6 miles	M	P	5 miles
C	F	5 miles	G	N	10 miles	N	P	4 miles
D	F	3 miles	H	L	2 miles	O	S	3 miles
D	G	3 miles	I	J	2 miles	P	S	4 miles
E	H	5 miles	I	L	3 miles			

Use with page 23.

Name

22

CYCLE THE DISTANCE, CONTINUED

Use with page 22.

1. Tom is considering three different paths to bike from point A to point L. Find the distance in miles for each path.

   I. A – D – F – J – L = 2 + 3 + 5 + 4 = _____ miles

   II. A – C – F – I – L = _____ miles

   III. A – B – E – H – L = _____ miles

2. If Tom bikes at a rate of 7 minutes per mile, calculate how long it will take him to cycle each of the three routes above.

   I. 14 miles x 7 minutes per mile = 98 minutes

   II. _____ miles x 7 minutes per mile = _____ minutes

   III. _____ miles x 7 minutes per mile = _____ minutes

3. Jane is considering three different routes from point A to point P. Calculate the miles for each route.

   I. A – B – E – I – J – M – P = _____ miles

   II. A – C – F – K – M – P = _____ miles

   III. A – D – G – N – P = _____ miles

4. Jane is able to ride at a speed of 1 mile every 6 minutes. Calculate her time for each of the 3 paths in question 3.

   I. _____ miles x 6 minutes per mile = _____ minutes

   II. _____ miles x 6 minutes per mile = _____ minutes

   III. _____ miles x 6 minutes per mile = _____ minutes

5. Find the shortest path in miles from point A to point S.

   I. Give the path in letters: A _____ S

   II. What is the length of the path in miles? _____ miles

6. If Jonathan rides at a speed of 1 mile every 5 minutes, how long will it take him to ride from point A to point S using the shortest route that you found in question five?

   _____

7. Every morning Jonathan regularly rides this route: D-F-I-E-C-A-D. How far does he ride each time?

   _____

Name _____

MOUNTAINS OF MEMORABILIA

Sarah, Jake, and Mark are great sports fans. They love to watch their favorite athletes and teams on TV or at live sporting events. But they also enjoy collecting memorabilia that was used by famous sports personalities or collectibles that commemorate their famous accomplishments.

1. Sarah has an interest in the Triple Crown of Racing: the Kentucky Derby, the Preakness Stakes, and the Belmont Stakes. She collects the official race day glasses from the three races and she also collects figurines of the horses that have won the races. Sarah has decided to total the value of the multiples in her collection.

Number in Collection	Description of the item	Value of one item	Total Value
5	1995 Kentucky Derby glass	$2	_____
3	1994 Triple Crown glasses (set)	$9	_____
7	1989 Belmont Stakes cups	$4	_____
4	Triple Crown horses (set)	$23	_____
8	Secretariat figurines	$6	_____
Total value			_____

2. Jake is a baseball fan, and his blood runs "Cincinnati Red." He collects rookie cards, signed baseballs, programs, and felt pennants.

Number in Collection	Description of the item	Value of one item	Total Value
9	Baseballs signed by Opening Day starters	$12	_____
6	Complete Rookie Card Sets (1995)	$29	_____
7	1994 World Series Programs	$5	_____
27	Felt Pennants 1993 (assorted teams)	$4	_____
3	Baseballs signed by Hal Morris	$7	_____
Total value			_____

3. Mark is a golfing fan. Since he hails from Georgia, his favorite tournament is the Masters at Augusta. His current favorite golfer is Tiger Woods.

Number in Collection	Description of the item	Value of one item	Total Value
5	Programs from the 1995 Masters	$3	_____
3	1996 Masters passes signed by Greg Norman	$14	_____
7	Golf balls used by Lee Trevino	$6	_____
2	Golf hats worn by Tiger Woods	$58	_____
9	Golf tees used by Tiger Woods	$2	_____
Total value			_____

Name

HOW MUCH IS ONE PLAYER WORTH?

Professional sports is a big money item. Star players or franchise players command multimillion dollar salaries that are paid out over several years. Below are some of the salaries negotiated and signed in 1996. Answer these questions about money earned by athletes.

_____ 1. Before being dethroned as the heavyweight boxing champion in a stunning upset by Evander Holyfield, Mike Tyson earned $75 million for three fights. On average, what did Mike earn per fight?

_____ 2. Alan Houston, who was coached by his father when he played basketball at the University of Tennessee, became a talented shooting guard in the NBA. The New York Knicks convinced him to sign a seven-year deal that was worth $56 million. On average, how much would Alan be earning per year?

_____ 3. Alonzo Mourning, nicknamed Zo by the media and his teammates, played his college hoops for John Thompson at Georgetown University. Under his new contract with the Miami Heat of the NBA he would be paid $112 million over the next seven years. How much would Zo be making on average each year?

_____ 4. Kenny Anderson signed a basketball contract with the Portland Trailblazers that would pay him $50 million over the next seven years. To the nearest dollar, how much would Kenny be paid on average for each of the next seven years?

_____ 5. The Seattle Mariners have one of the premier shortstops in major league baseball in Alex Rodriguez. Under a recent contract he would be paid $105 million over the next three years. On average, how much would Alex's yearly salary be?

_____ 6. The high scorer among the Washington Bullets for the 1995–1996 season was Juwan Howard with 1789 points. His contract stipulated that he would be paid $105 million over the next seven years. How much is Juwan's average annual salary?

_____ 7. The Atlanta Hawks of the NBA have been pleased with the play of Dikembe Mutumbo. He signed a five-year contract with them that would pay him a total of $50 million. Compute his average yearly salary in millions of dollars.

_____ 8. The Los Angeles Lakers convinced Shaquille O'Neal to leave the Orlando Magic by paying him over $120 million dollars. Since the Shaq weighed in at 300 pounds, how much did Los Angeles pay per pound for this marquee player?

9. Michael Jordan, who many consider the greatest basketball player ever, signed a one-year contract with the Chicago Bulls for $25 million.

_____ a. Although the regular season is 82 games long, the Bulls would almost certainly be in the playoffs again. Assuming that they could play as many as 100 games in all, calculate what the Bulls would be paying Michael for each game.

_____ b. In the 1995–1996 basketball season, Michael scored 2491 points. If he scored 2500 points in the next season, how much would he be earning per point?

Name _____

QUOTE ME!

One of the greatest slogans of sports is:

> " What matters is not the size of the dog in the fight, but the size of the fight in the dog! "

To discover who made this statement, work each exercise below. Each time the answer appears, write the matching letter below it.

$7\overline{)630}$	$8\overline{)5600}$	$24\overline{)72}$	$53\overline{)424}$	$12\overline{)48}$	$91\overline{)819}$	$44\overline{)264}$
C	T	O	N	A	Y	H

$12\overline{)7584}$	$41\overline{)31,734}$	$31\overline{)899}$	$65\overline{)780}$	$24\overline{)744}$	$41\overline{)902}$
R	P	U	L	B	E

90   3   4   90   6   774   4   29   12

___ ___ ___ ___ ___   ___ ___ ___ ___

" 31   22   4   632 "   31   632   9   4   8   700

___ ___ ___ ___ ___   ___ ___ ___ ___ ___ ___

Name _____

DIVIDE THE SAVINGS

Here's a quick review of some divisibility rules. You'll need them to solve the problems below.

If a number is divisible by:

    . . . 2, then the ones digit is even

    . . . 3, then the sum of the digits is divisible by 3

    . . . 4, then the number formed by the last two digits is divisible by 4

    . . . 5, then the ones digit is 0 or 5

    . . . 6, then the number is divisible by 2 and 3

    . . . 10, then the ones digit is 0

The Goal Post Sports Store is having a Midnight Madness Sale. Read the ad and answer the questions that follow.

MIDNIGHT MADNESS SALE

MEN'S SUPER TENNIS SHOES $15.00

FOOTBALL T-SHIRTS ONLY $12.00

PRO TEAM CAPS $4.45 !!

aqua shoes $17.00

TIGER GOLF CLUBS $150.00

Soccer Shoes $25.00

We pay all sales tax during this sale!

____ 1. Could you pay for the Men's New Super Tennis Shoes with all five-dollar bills and receive no change back?

____ 2. If you wanted the football T-Shirt and the Aqua Shoes, could you pay with all ten-dollar bills and receive no change back?

____ 3. If you had only nickels, could you pay for the Pro Team Cap and receive no change back?

____ 4. If six friends wanted to buy a set of Tiger Golf Clubs together, could they split the bill evenly with no one having to pay extra?

____ 5. If four sisters wanted to buy their father a pair of Aqua Shoes, a pair of Men's New Super Tennis Shoes, and a football T-Shirt, could they split the bill evenly with no one having to pay extra?

Using the divisibility rules above, determine whether each number is divisible by 2, 3, 4, 5, 6, or 10. If it is divisible by a number, place an X in the appropriate row.

	58	153	228	523	80	104	180	89	532	90
2										
3										
4										
5										
6										
10										

Name

PRIME-TIME SCOREBOARD

This scoreboard changes images during intermissions and other breaks. When it's not showing the score, it's showing a message to the crowd. Shade in all the prime numbers with a red marker and shade all composite numbers with a blue marker to read the message it's flashing today.

FOOTBALL MATCHUPS

Athletes are often given nicknames. Here are some nicknames of some famous football players. To match the nicknames with the athletes, find the letter (A–J) that matches the exponential number (1–10).

____ 1. 5^4 Deion Sanders

____ 2. 4^3 Jeff Hostetler

____ 3. 1^{40} Willie Anderson

____ 4. 2^5 REGGIE WHITE

____ 5. 13^2 DESMOND HOWARD

____ 6. 8^3 Red Grange

____ 7. 9^4 John Riggins

____ 8. 6^1 Andy Nelson

____ 9. 7^2 Fred Evans

____ 10. 6^4 BART BUETOW

A.	64	Hoss
B.	32	The Minister Of Defense
C.	6561	The Diesel
D.	625	Prime Time
E.	6	Bones
F.	49	Dippy
G.	1	Flipper
H.	169	Magic
I.	1296	The Mad Scientist
J.	512	The Galloping Ghost

SUPER STAR PROBLEMS

Find the value of each expression.

11. $2^3 \cdot 7^2$ _____

12. $5^2 \cdot 8^2 \cdot 3^3$ _____

13. 100^3 _____

14. $5 \cdot 6^3 \cdot 10^3$ _____

15. $3^2 \cdot 4^3$ _____

16. $5^3 \cdot 100^2$ _____

17. $2^2 \cdot 7^2$ _____

18. $5^0 \cdot 5^2$ _____

19. $9^2 \cdot 2^2 \cdot 3^2$ _____

20. $10 \cdot 4 \cdot 6^2$ _____

21. $25^2 \cdot 2^3$ _____

22. $4^2 \cdot 10^2$ _____

Name _____

29

Basic Skills/Whole Numbers & Integers 6-8+   Copyright ©1997 by Incentive Publications, Inc., Nashville, TN

THREE KEYS TO SPORTS SUCCESS

Nick knows that great ability at running, jumping, and throwing are the keys to success in many sports. As a trivia fan, he likes to keep up with the running, jumping, and throwing records set by both man and beast. The following facts are some that Nick finds most interesting. See how many you know.

_____ 1. Michael Johnson won gold medals in the men's 200 m and 400 m sprints at the 1996 Olympic Games held in Atlanta. Write 200 m and 400 m as powers of ten.

_____ 2. In a tournament situation, one of the best Frisbee™ throwers in the world tossed the Frisbee™ 500 feet or 6000 inches. Write these two distances as powers of ten.

_____ 3. One of the fastest land animals is the cheetah, which has been clocked at speeds of 100,000 mm per hour. Write this rate as a power of ten.

_____ 4. The men's water-ski jumping record is over 6×10^1 m or 6×10^4 mm. Write these two distances without using powers of ten.

_____ 5. The men's Olympic high jump record was set by American Charles Austin at the Atlanta games with a mark of 2.39×10^3 mm. The long jump record is still held by American Bob Beamon with a jump of 8.9×10^2 cm which he set at the Mexico Olympics. Write these two distances without using powers of ten.

_____ 6. The Olympic record in the marathon is held by Carlos Lopes of Portugal and was set at the Los Angeles Olympics with a time of 7761 seconds. Round these seconds to the nearest thousand and write them as a power of ten.

_____ 7. A marathon race is 26 miles and 385 yards long. It commemorates a Greek messenger's run from the city of Marathon to Athens to proclaim a great victory over the Persians. This distance in yards is 46,145. Round this number to the nearest ten thousand and write it as a power of ten.

8. Secretariat was one of the greatest horses ever to win the triple crown. His record winning time for the Kentucky Derby was 119.4 seconds (set in 1973). The distance for the Derby race is 2310 yards.

_____ a. Round the time to the nearest ten and write it as a power of ten.

_____ b. Round the distance to the nearest hundred and write as a power of ten.

_____ 9. The highest jump by any animal is an estimated thirty-foot leap by a Mako shark. This height in millimeters would be about 9414. Round this number to the nearest thousand and write it as a power of ten.

_____ 10. The Olympic record in the javelin was set in 1976 by Miklos Nemeth of Hungary with a throw of 9.458×10^4 mm. Round this distance to the nearest thousand and write it without using a power of ten.

Name _____

ERRANDS ON SKIS

Anne has been snowed in at the cabin for several days. She wants to plan a trip so that when she is able to get out she can run all of her errands and get back to the cabin using the shortest route. She has a diagram of the area (not drawn to scale).

Below are the distances measured from a map. These distances need to be converted to yards. The scale of the map is 1 mm = 100 yards and 1 cm = 1000 yards.

C = cabin
D = drugstore
G = grocery
R = restaurant
S = ski lodge
V = video store

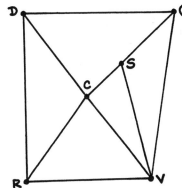

CR = 9.2 mm
VG = 1.4 cm
CD = 6.8 mm
VR = 2.7 cm
CS = 8.9 mm
VS = 3.1 cm
CV = 7.3 mm
SG = 8.7 cm
DR = 9.5 cm
GD = 10.6 cm

Convert the above measurements to yards.

1. Cabin to restaurant_____

2. Cabin to drugstore _____

3. Cabin to ski lodge _____

4. Cabin to video store _____

5. Drugstore to restaurant _____

6. Video store to grocery_____

7. Video store to restaurant _____

8. Video store to ski lodge_____

9. Ski lodge to grocery _____

10. Grocery to drugstore _____

Find the shortest route in yards that begins at the cabin, visits each site once, and returns to the cabin. Describe the shortest route and give its distance in yards.

11. Route _____

_____

_____

_____

_____

_____

_____

12. Length of route in yards _____

Name _____

RACING RATES

Nakia has the need for speed. She loves things that are fast. Her fascination has led her to read everything she can find about speeds achieved in air, on water, and on land. Here are some facts that she has found. Convert each to kilometers per hour.

_____ 1. Parachutists can reach speeds of 298,000 meters per hour in a skydiving free fall. Divide this number by 1000 to find out the parachutist's speed in kph.

_____ 2. Racing pigeons flying in windless conditions have achieved speeds of 9.7×10^6 centimeters per hour. Divide this speed by 100,000 to find the pigeon's speed in kph.

_____ 3. In 1976 an official world air speed record was set by a jet plane traveling 3,529,560 meters per hour. Divide the jet's speed by 10^3 to find the rate in kph.

_____ 4. An unofficial world record was set in water skiing in 1979 when a speed of 2.06×10^8 millimeters per hour was measured. Divide this rate by one million to find its rate in kph.

_____ 5. In 1977 an unlimited hydroplane set an unofficial world water speed record by traveling at a speed of 55,600 dekameters. Dividing by a hundred will give the speed in kph.

_____ 6. A board sailing world mark was set in 1980 when a speed of 4.5 million centimeters per hour was recorded. To find the rate in kph divide by 100,000.

_____ 7. The world speed record for ice yachting was set in 1938 when a speed of 2.3×10^6 decimeters per hour was reached. The rate in kph can be found by dividing by 10,000.

_____ 8. Craig Breedlove hopes to bring the world land speed record for jet-powered vehicles back to the United States. He is developing a new vehicle called the Spirit of America that he hopes will break the sound barrier by traveling at a rate of 1.224 million meters per hour. By dividing this number by 10^3 the rate in kph can be found.

_____ 9. The top speeds achieved by skateboarders in a standing position are so fast that they would outpace both speed skaters and racehorses. A world speed record set in 1978 clocked the rate of a standing skateboarder to be 8.6 million centimeters per hour. Divide this speed by 100,000 to find the answer in kph.

10. If the previous 9 speedsters were to be ranked by their speeds in kph, put a rank beside them where 1 would be the fastest and 9 would be the slowest.

☐ Parachutist	☐ Water skier	☐ Ice yacht
☐ Racing pigeon	☐ Hydroplane	☐ Jet vehicle
☐ Jet plane	☐ Board sailer	☐ Skate boarder

Name _____

PROBLEMS WITH WHEELS

Biking is one of the fastest growing and most popular sports around the country for competition and for recreation. Solve these problems about folks on wheels.

_____ 1. Almost 100,000 bike riders are members of the League of American Cyclists. If the club magazine is bundled in packages of 10, how many bundles will there be to mail?

_____ 2. The bicycle was introduced to the United States in 1866. How many years ago did this happen?

_____ 3. In 1983, Laurent Fignon won the Tour de France in a little more than 105 hours. If the race was 2,315 miles long, what was his average speed per hour?

A bicycle store is having a sale. Using the sales flier at right, solve the following problems.

_____ 4. Mark wants a new 10-speed bike, a deluxe helmet, and a water bottle. What is his total bill?

_____ 5. Evan is trying to watch his budget. He decides to buy a rebuilt 3-speed bike, a basic helmet, handle grips, and a water bottle. What is his total bill?

_____ 6. Abby wants a new 3-speed bike and a deluxe helmet. The bike store owner will take her old bike as a trade-in. How much will she owe the bike store if the owner gives her $50 for her old bike?

Cycle City

Spring Sale

NEW 10-SPEED BIKES: $350.00

NEW 3-SPEED BIKES: $200.00

REBUILT BIKES
10-SPEED $175.00
3-SPEED $100.00

DELUXE HELMETS: $75.00

BASIC HELMETS: $25.00

HANDLE GRIPS: $15.00

WATER BOTTLES: only....$5.00

_____ 7. Ramon wants to buy a new 10-speed bike, a basic helmet, and a water bottle. He doesn't have enough money now, but the owner says he will put these items on lay away for him. To place these items on layaway it will cost an additional $10. What is his total bill? He wants to pay in 3 installments for the items. How much will he have to pay each time?

_____ 8. Hilary works at the bike store and receives $25 off on any item she buys over $50. If she wants to buy a new 3-speed bike and a basic helmet, how much is her total bill?

Name _____

RIVER TRIP

Sam's dad has offered to take him on a trip to a river lodge. Sam is allowed to bring David and Mike with him if the three friends will split their expenses. Solve the problems on this page and the next (page 35) about their trip.

_____ 1. On the way to the river Sam's dad fills the car with gas and the bill comes to $22. If he contributes $7, how much will each of the three boys need to pay for gas?

_____ 2. At dinner, each of the boys orders separately. Sam's hamburger platter and milkshake comes to $6. David's chicken sandwich, onion rings, and drink cost $7. Mike's spaghetti, milk, and pie total $8. If Sam's dad gathers the money and pays the total bill with $30, then how much did his dinner cost?

_____ 3. At the lodge, the three boys share a room. The charge for Thursday night's stay will be $75, but the room rate for Friday and Saturday is $93 a night. What is the total room charge for their three-night stay, and what is each boy's share of the bill?

_____ 4. On Friday morning Sam's dad treats the boys to a pancake breakfast and asks what their plans are for the day. David outlines the boys' plans below.

TIME:	ACTIVITY:	CHARGES:	COST:
9:00 – 11:00	Mountain biking	$4. per bike	_____
11:00 – 12:00	Swimming	no charge	_____
12:00 – 1:00	Picnic with Ice cream	$14. total	_____
1:00 – 2:00	Water sliding	$6. each	_____
2:00 – 3:00	Jet Skiing	$100. total	_____
3:00 – 4:00	Basketball	no charge	_____
4:00 – 5:00	Video games	$3. each	_____
5:00 – 6:00	Buffet dinner	$25. total	_____
6:00 – 7:30	Bowling	$9. each	_____
7:30 – 9:30	Watching movies	$5. total	_____

_____ a. Give the total amount that the three boys will owe for the day if they participate in all of these activities.

_____ b. Give the share for each boy.

Use with page 35.

Name

RIVER TRIP, CONTINUED

Use with page 34.

_____ 5. On Saturday, Sam's dad offers to treat the boys to a float trip on the river.

If innertube rental with life jacket and insurance is $14 per person, round-trip transportation is $5 per person, and the picnic at the waterfall is $7 per person, what will the trip for four cost? If Sam's dad pays with two fifties and a twenty, how much change should he receive?

_____ 6. After dinner, the three friends decide to take a river cruise featuring fire-works and a beach bonfire hosted by the lodge's entertainment staff. If the cost is $14 per person, how much will David and Mike have to pay if they decide to pay Sam's way?

_____ 7. At breakfast on Sunday, the three friends decide to treat Sam's dad to the lodge's special brunch buffet. If the cost is $12 per person, how much will each boy have to pay to settle the bill for four if a $6 tip is added?

_____ 8. After the Sunday brunch, the three friends pool their remaining cash. It totals $31. Kayak rental with helmet, paddle, and life vest is $13 per person for a half day. How much will they need to borrow from Sam's dad to be able to kayak?

_____ 9. On the way home, Sam's dad reminds the boys that they have not saved any money to pay for gas and dinner on the way home. By the time they get home from the river, the boys are in debt to dad for $36. If he offers to pay each boy $2 an hour for yard work, how many hours will each of the three friends need to work for Sam's dad to pay off their river trip?

10. When the boys go to develop their pictures, they find that they have each taken 6 rolls of 36 pictures each.

_____ a. How many pictures will they have to have developed?

_____ b. If each boy spends $48, how much will each picture cost to develop?

Name _____

GEARING UP

While surfing the Internet, Will found a store that sold authentic team wear. He printed the price list. Study the prices and then estimate the cost of the items that he may purchase. Solve all problems on this page and the next page (page 37).

HOME AND AWAY JACKET
(MANY NBA, MLB, NHL, NFL, and NCAA TEAM JACKETS AVAILABLE)
Child – M,L – $89.99
Adult – S, M, – $119.99
L, XL – $129.99
XXL –

AUTHENTIC NFL TURF SHIRT
(ALL NFL TEAMS)
Adult Sizes:
S, M, L, XL, XXL, 3XL
$29.99

NFL PRO JERSEY
(Inquire for teams/players available.)
Adult: S,M,L – $109.99
Adult: 46, 48, 50, 52 – $189.99

SHADOW CAP
[MANY NFL AND NCAA TEAMS AVAILABLE.]
ADJUSTABLE
$19.99

PRO JACKETS
[MANY NFL AND NCAA AVAILABLE.]
Child: S,M, L – $94.99
Adult: S,M, L, XL – $119.99
XXL – $129.99

HOODED SWEATSHIRTS
[many NFL, MLB, NHL, NCAA teams available.]
Adult only: S, M, L, XL, XXL
$39.99

Shipping Information:
Add: $5.99 for orders under $50.
$7.99 for orders $50.-$100.
$9.99 for orders over $100.
(Florida Residents Add 7% sales tax)

1. When Will found this site he told his mom about it. She suggested that he determine approximately how much it would cost to buy his family hooded sweatshirts. His family included the following members:

Family Member	Adult Size	Favorite Team
Dad	XXL	Oilers
Mom	L	Oilers
Claire (sister)	S	Giants
Eric (brother)	M	Steelers
Will	M	Vikings

About how much would it cost to buy one sweatshirt for each person and pay for the shipping?

Use with page 37.

Name

GEARING UP, CONTINUED

Use with page 36.

2. It's hard to buy presents for Grandpa. He is an XXL and enjoys the 49ers. Mom told Will that he could order Grandpa's Christmas presents if he did not spend more than $120. Write two estimated orders for Grandpa and don't forget to include the shipping charges.

3. Will loves authentic team wear. He was wondering how much it would cost to buy one of every item for himself. About how much would it cost for Will to order everything that the sport store has in Viking sportswear?

4. Will has drawn his cousin's name in the family gift exchange. The price limit for the gift is around $25. What could Will buy for his cousin with this budget?

5. Uncle Mark is a former linebacker for the Chicago Bears. His is 6'4" tall and weighs 350 pounds. He is a size 52 or 3XL. Mom told Will to order Uncle Mark one of whatever the store has in his size with the Chicago Bears emblem on it. What could he order, and about how much would this cost?

6. Will's community center has a football team called the Wildcats. About how much would it cost to buy all 25 members of the team turf shirts with Wildcats embroidered on them?

7. Will's grandma always gives him $100 for his birthday. Write up two estimated orders that Will might want to purchase.

8. Nicole came over to Will's house dressed in her favorite team clothing. She has on a home-and-away jacket (size S), a turf shirt, and a shadow cap. About how much did her ensemble cost?

9. Nicole then told Will that her grandmother, who lives in Florida, bought her the outfit. About how much did her ensemble cost her grandmother?

Name

PUTTIN' ON THE DOG

Margie enjoys working with her three dogs to show at kennel club events. She has raised Beau, the beagle, from a pup and prefers to enter him in the obstacle course event. Simon, the Scottie, has a gentle temperament and minds well. He excels in the discipline events. Connie, the cocker spaniel, has personality and loves to show off. She performs well in the show dog classes. Help Margie solve the following problems to successfully prepare and compete in the dog show. (See if you can find out what the expression used in the title of this page means.)

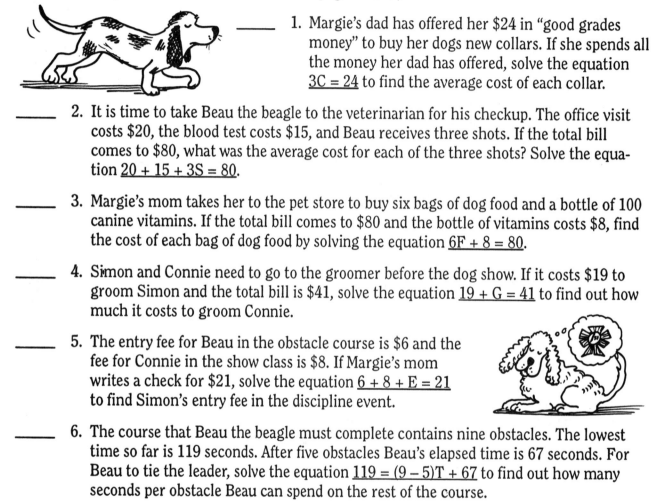

_____ 1. Margie's dad has offered her $24 in "good grades money" to buy her dogs new collars. If she spends all the money her dad has offered, solve the equation $3C = 24$ to find the average cost of each collar.

_____ 2. It is time to take Beau the beagle to the veterinarian for his checkup. The office visit costs $20, the blood test costs $15, and Beau receives three shots. If the total bill comes to $80, what was the average cost for each of the three shots? Solve the equation $20 + 15 + 3S = 80$.

_____ 3. Margie's mom takes her to the pet store to buy six bags of dog food and a bottle of 100 canine vitamins. If the total bill comes to $80 and the bottle of vitamins costs $8, find the cost of each bag of dog food by solving the equation $6F + 8 = 80$.

_____ 4. Simon and Connie need to go to the groomer before the dog show. If it costs $19 to groom Simon and the total bill is $41, solve the equation $19 + G = 41$ to find out how much it costs to groom Connie.

_____ 5. The entry fee for Beau in the obstacle course is $6 and the fee for Connie in the show class is $8. If Margie's mom writes a check for $21, solve the equation $6 + 8 + E = 21$ to find Simon's entry fee in the discipline event.

_____ 6. The course that Beau the beagle must complete contains nine obstacles. The lowest time so far is 119 seconds. After five obstacles Beau's elapsed time is 67 seconds. For Beau to tie the leader, solve the equation $119 = (9 - 5)T + 67$ to find out how many seconds per obstacle Beau can spend on the rest of the course.

_____ 7. Simon the Scottie received seven scores of eight and three scores of six from the ten judges at the discipline event. If the top dog got a score of 93, solve the equation $93 = (7 \times 8) + (3 \times 6) + D$ to find out how many points out of first place Simon fell.

_____ 8. In the spaniel class there were 36 entries. If the total number of spaniels in the class was nine times as many as the number of dogs that placed better than Connie (in the judge's opinion), solve the equation $36 = 9 (P - 1)$ to find out what place Connie took in the competition.

Name

GO FLY A KITE

Jessica and Gina find that kite flying is great exercise. They've decided to build their own kite. They have instructions for building the following types of kites: a three-foot box kite, a six-foot delta wing kite, and a two-foot traditional kite.

_____ 1. Jessica's brother gives the girls three yards of kite-making material, but they need seven yards total. Write an equation to find "M," the material they will need to buy.

_____ 2. If Jessica and Gina decide to buy four yards of material and spend $24, write an equation to find "P," the price per yard of the kite-making material.

_____ 3. The girls saved $60 to spend on their kite project. After spending $24 on material, write an equation to find "L," the money they have left to finish the project.

4. The hobby store sells the special wooden dowels for making kites at $2 per four-foot dowel. Gina has determined that they will need 48 feet of wood to make their three kites.

_____ a. Write an equation to find "D," the number of four-foot wooden dowels needed.

_____ b. Write an equation to find "W," the cost of the wood.

_____ 5. Jessica calculates that 300 feet of kite string will be needed. Write an equation to find "B," how many balls of string should be purchased if each ball contains 75 feet of string.

_____ 6. Jessica's mom says that "twice the height of the kite minus 100 is equal to the length of string that is let out" is an equation that can be used to calculate the approximate height of the kite. Write an equation to calculate the kite's maximum height "H" if all 300 feet of kite string are let out.

_____ 7. A traditional kite should have a tail that is twice as long as its length. If Gina has a kite tail that is six feet long, write an equation to find "K," the maximum length of the traditional kite with which it could be used.

_____ 8. Jessica thinks the delta wing kite flies best when the wind blows at least 15 miles per hour. Write an equation to calculate "R," the speed at which Jessica should run if the wind is blowing at 11 mph.

Name _____

Basic Skills/Whole Numbers & Integers 6-8+

THE BIG GUYS OF THE NBA

Not only are they tall—really tall—but their scores are tall as well. Here are some of the leading scorers in the NBA, and some of their scores from one basketball season. Use the information on the chart to answer the questions below.

	Field Goals	Free Throws	Points	Average Points
Michael Jordan	916	548	2,491	30
H. Olajuwon	768	397	1,936	27
SHAQUILLE O'NEAL	592	249	1,434	27
Karl Malone	789	512	2,106	26
David Robinson	711	626	2,051	25
Charles Barkley	580	440	1,649	23
Patrick Ewing	678	351	1,711	23
Grant Hill	564	485	1,618	20
Scottie Pippin	563	220	1,496	19
A. Hardaway	623	445	1,780	22

1. To determine how many more field goals Michael Jordan has than any other player, would you add, subtract, multiply, or divide? _____

2. To total up the number of points earned by Jordan, O'Neal, and Barkley, would you add, subtract, multiply, or divide?

3. A statistician determined the number of points each player averaged per game. How do you think the statistician was able to determine the average points of the players?

_____

4. How many more points must Grant Hill score to catch up with Michael Jordan? _____

5. Scottie Pippin and Michael Jordan play for Chicago. Shaquille O'Neal and A. Hardaway used to play for Orlando. If both players on both teams had played an average game and they were the only players to score, would Chicago or Orlando have won? What would be the final score? _____

6. Which player leads in field goals? How many more field goals does he have than any other player? _____

7. Which player leads in free throws? How many more free throws does he have than any other player?

_____

_____

8. Which player leads in points? How many more points does he have than any other player?

_____

_____

9. If you wanted to determine how many points were earned by all the players in the chart, would you add, subtract, multiply, or divide?

_____

10. Write three story problems that could be solved by using the chart of basketball statistics.

Name _____

FOLLOW THE CLUES

Follow the clues to find the name of the answer that matches each description (1–8). Pay attention to the integers written next to each athlete's name on the chart.

	Integer	Athlete			Integer	Athlete
A.	–16	Kerri Strug		E.	–2	Cigar
B.	+8	Evander Holyfield		F.	4	Joe Montana
C.	–6	Shaquille O'Neal		G.	–8	Emmit Smith
D.	0	Penny Hardaway		H.	10	Juwan Howard

_____ 1. This integer is greater than –20 but less than –12.
The athlete it represents is a famous gymnast that completed a final vault with a wrenched ankle to assist her team in winning a gold medal.

_____ 2. This integer is positive and is less than 7.
The athlete it represents was named Most Valuable Player in Super Bowls XVI, XIX, and XXIV.

_____ 3. This integer is greater than 9 and less than 15.
The athlete is 6'8" and received $105 million to play professional basketball.

_____ 4. This integer is greater than –2 but less than 1.
The athlete is an NBA player who drives a white Ferrari with a small "¢" embedded in gold on the hood.

_____ 5. This integer is greater than –3 but less than –1.
This is a horse that won 16 consecutive victories from October 1994 to August 1996.

_____ 6. This integer is greater than 4 but less than 9.
This athlete beat Mike Tyson in 1996.

_____ 7. This integer is greater than –9 but less than –6.
This athlete rushed 1,563 yards for the Dallas Cowboys.

_____ 8. This integer is greater than –7 but less than –4.
This athlete made a deal with the L.A. Lakers to earn $121 million over 7 years.

Name

PRESIDENTIAL GOLF

Many doctors and other experts agree that participating in sports is a great way to reduce stress. Lots of folks also agree that the most stressful job in the United States is that of president. Of the 16 presidents between William Taft and Bill Clinton, only three did not play golf (Hoover, Truman, and Carter). Below is the scorecard from a fictional golf game the presidents played against three leading golf pros. Review their scores, and then answer the questions on the next page (page 43).

Golf Scoring

- To play at par is to use the same number of strokes as the assigned par value and is scored as a 0.
- If a golfer uses 2 strokes more than the assigned par, the score is +2.
- Good golfers can use fewer strokes than the assigned par value. To play 1 stroke under par is scored –1.

President	Score	Par	+ or – Par
John F. Kennedy	80	72	+ 8
D. Eisenhower	79	72	+ 7
Gerald Ford	81	72	+ 9
Franklin Roosevelt	89	72	+17
Ronald Reagan	90	72	+18
Richard Nixon	92	72	+20
George Bush	81	72	+ 9
Bill Clinton	90	72	+18
William Taft	69	72	– 3
Warren Harding	100	72	+28
Woodrow Wilson	115	72	+43
Lyndon Johnson	101	72	+29
Calvin Coolidge	120	72	+48

Professional Golfers	Score	Par	+ or – Par
Tiger Woods	65	72	–7
Greg Norman	64	72	–8
Tom Watson	68	72	–4

TAKE COVER, IKE. I'M PLAYING THROUGH!

RIGHT-O, TAFT.

Use with page 43.

Name

PRESIDENTIAL GOLF, CONTINUED

Use with page 42.

1. On the number line plot Gerald Ford's, William Taft's, D. Eisenhower's, Bill Clinton's, Tiger Wood's, Greg Norman's, and Tom Watson's strokes above (+) or below (–) par.

Score	62	64	66	68	70	72	74	76	78	80	82	84	86	88	90	92
+ or – Par	–10	–8	–6	–4	–2	0	2	4	6	8	10	12	14	16	18	20

2. Plot Tiger Woods' and John F. Kennedy's scores in relation to par 72 at 0 on the number line below.

Score	62	64	66	68	70	72	74	76	78	80	82	84	86	88	90	92
+ or – Par	–10	–8	–6	–4	–2	0	2	4	6	8	10	12	14	16	18	20

3. Calvin Coolidge was the least competent of all presidential golfers. On one hole he took 11 strokes to complete a par 3. Plot his strokes above par for this hole on the number line below. How many strokes above par was President Coolidge?

Score	1	2	3	4	5	6	7	8	9	10	11	12	13
+ or – Par	–2	–1	0	1	2	3	4	5	6	7	8	9	10

4. Woodrow and Edith Wilson often golfed together between 5 and 6 A.M. On a par 5, Edith's score was 4 and Woodrow's score was 7. Plot each of their scores in relation to par at zero.

Score	1	2	3	4	5	6	7	8	9	10
+ or – Par	–4	–3	–2	–1	0	1	2	3	4	5

5. President Clinton is known for taking mulligans. A mulligan is a golf shot that you get to "do over." By liberally using mulligans, Clinton scored an 80 one day when playing with Tom Watson. Tom Watson scored a 68. Plot each of their scores in relation to a par 72 at 0. How many shots separated the two golfers?

Score	62	64	66	68	70	72	74	76	78	80	82	84	86	88	90	92
+ or – Par	–10	–8	–6	–4	–2	0	2	4	6	8	10	12	14	16	18	20

• George Bush liked to play rapidly. He played 18 holes with a foursome in 1 hour and 42 minutes.

Did You Know?....

• William H. Taft weighed 355 pounds, but was a respectable golfer.
• Warren G. Harding spent Election Day in 1920 golfing in knickers and an old red sweater at Scioto Country Club in Columbus, Ohio.
• It was said that Lyndon B. Johnson "went to the ball as though he were killing a snake."

Name _____

DO YOU KNOW YOUR VENUES?

A **venue** is a location where something takes place. This word is used to describe the setting for Olympic events. The puzzle below will reveal venues of the Olympic Games in 1904, 1920, and 1932. First, you need to solve the integer problems to find the number that fits each letter. Then, write the letter on the line to match each letter in the puzzle.
Solve the problems below to find which letter is paired with each answer.

[A] $-8 - (-9) =$ ____

[B] $+5 + (+4) =$ ____

[C] $+(-6) - (+9) =$ ____

[D] $+12 + (-9) =$ ____

[E] $(-3) + (-5) =$ ____

[F] $(+23) - (+9) =$ ____

[G] $-(+13) - (-7) =$ ____

[H] $+(-11) - (+5) =$ ____

[I] $-(-2) + (-7) =$ ____

[J] $-11 + (+7) =$ ____

[K] $-5 + (-7) =$ ____

[L] $+13 + (-8) =$ ____

[M] $-(-3) + (+14) =$ ____

[N] $-6 + (+22) =$ ____

[O] $(-9) - (+8) =$ ____

[P] $-(-14) + (-17) =$ ____

[Q] $+(+4) - (-8) =$ ____

[R] $-(+18) + (+4) =$ ____

[S] $-1 + (+7) =$ ____

[T] $-9 - (+12) =$ ____

[U] $-(-15) - (+8) =$ ____

[V] $+6 + (-24) =$ ____

[W] $(+6) + (+9) =$ ____

[X] $-(+25) + (+12) =$ ____

[Y] $+(+18) - (+5) =$ ____

[Z] $-(-6) - (-12) =$ ____

[Blank] $(-4) + (-7) =$ ____

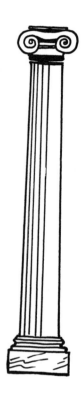

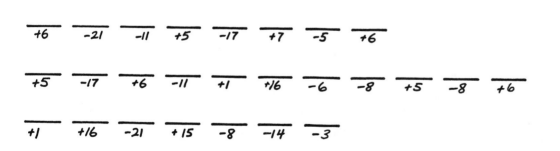

+6 -21 -11 +5 -17 +7 -5 +6

+5 -17 +6 -11 +1 +16 -6 -8 +5 -8 +6

+1 +16 -21 +15 -8 -14 -3

Name ____

IT HELPS TO SPEAK LATIN

Although the ancient Greeks held Olympic games every four years beginning around 776 B.C., the modern Olympic games have been around only since A.D.1896. At that time a French educator decided to invite young athletes from around the world to Athens to begin the modern Olympic games. While the Summer Olympics are now held in the years divisible by four and the Winter Olympics are held in even numbered years not divisible by four, the Olympic motto is still the same. The motto in Latin is "Citius, Altius, Fortius." Use the integer problems and alphabet key below to find (1) the last name of the French educator Baron Pierre de _____ , who began the modern Olympic games, and (2) the English translation for the Olympic motto.

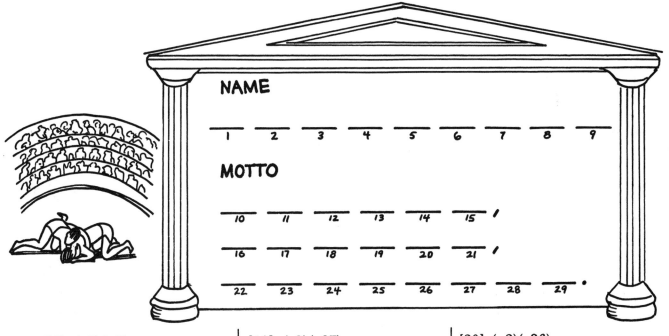

[1] $(-7)(+7)$ = _____

[2] $(+6)(-6)$ = _____

[3] $(-5)(-13)$ = _____

[4] $(-4)(-9)$ = _____

[5] $(-8)(+9)$ = _____

[6] $(+8)(-7)$ = _____

[7] $(+8)(+6)$ = _____

[8] $(-9)(+6)$ = _____

[9] $(-4)(-5)$ = _____

[10] $(-3)(-27)$ = _____

[11] $(-3)(+14)$ = _____

[12] $(-3)(-24)$ = _____

[13] $(+3)(+16)$ = _____

[14] $(+12)(-6)$ = _____

[15] $(-4)(+14)$ = _____

[16] $(-6)(-7)$ = _____

[17] $(+3)(-18)$ = _____

[18] $(-15)(0)$ = _____

[19] $(+2)(+21)$ = _____

[20] $(+2)(-36)$ = _____

[21] $(-2)(+28)$ = _____

[22] $(-6)(-12)$ = _____

[23] $(-8)(-6)$ = _____

[24] $(-8)(+7)$ = _____

[25] $(+12)(-3)$ = _____

[26] $(-2)(-10)$ = _____

[27] $(+16)(0)$ = _____

[28] $(-18)(+4)$ = _____

[29] $(-14)(+4)$ = _____

Alphabet for Matching Answers to Letters

A = –42	B = +36	C = –49	D = –65	E = –72	F = +81	G = 0	H = +42	I = –54
J = –81	K = +24	L = –50	M = –64	N = +20	O = –36	P = +32	Q = –18	R = –56
S = +72	T = +48	U = +65	V = –32	W = –24	X = +18	Y = +64	Z = –45	

Name

DOES PRACTICE MAKE PERFECT?

They say that "practice makes perfect" in sports, in hobbies, and in physical or mental activity—even in math. Do you think this is always a true saying? See if you can get a perfect score practicing the multiplication of integers.

1. 7 • 9

2. –7 • –9

3. 7 • –9

4. –7 • 9

5. 7 • 3

6. –7 • 3

7. 7 • –3

8. –7 • –3

9. 2 • 11

10. –2 • 11

11. 2 • –11

12. –2 • –11

13. 18 • 10

14. –18 • 10

15. –18 • –10

16. 18 • –10

17. 33 • 20

18. –33 • 20

19. 33 • –20

20. –33 • –20

Complete each chart below.

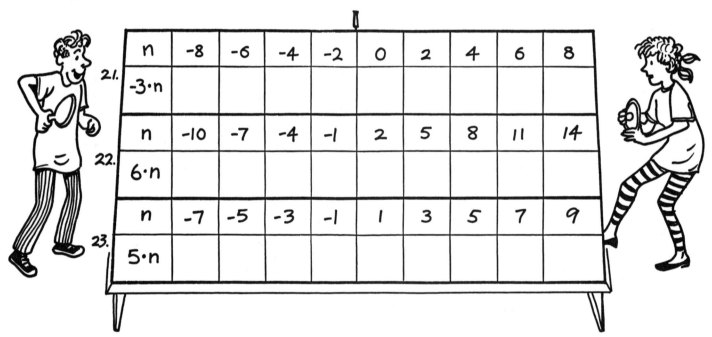

n	-8	-6	-4	-2	0	2	4	6	8
21. -3·n									

n	-10	-7	-4	-1	2	5	8	11	14
22. 6·n									

n	-7	-5	-3	-1	1	3	5	7	9
23. 5·n									

Without multiplying, tell if the product is positive (write +) or negative (write –).

_____ 24. –6 • 8 • –3

_____ 25. –7 • 4 • –6

_____ 26. –8 • –3 • –3 • 9

Find the products of the following:

_____ 27. 8 • –2 • –4

_____ 28. –7 • –2 • –5 • 7

_____ 29. –10 • 0 • 100 • 1

_____ 30. 234 • –25 • 2

Name

MYSTERY NAME

This mystery athlete turned professional as a twenty-year-old. In his first year as a pro he earned $60 million in endorsements. Besides being named the top amateur in his sport for three years in a row, he won two professional tournaments in the first seven that he entered, beating both Payne Stewart and Davis Love III. Although he did not win the first Skins Game he played as a professional, he did prove that he could drive the ball as far as John Daly. Many predict that he will win a green jacket before Greg Norman. The letters of this athlete's name are scrambled in the grid below. Follow the directions in this worksheet to find out how to reveal the name.

FIRST, work the problems.

(a) $-36 / -6 =$ _____

(b) $0 / +9 =$ _____

(c) $-64 / +8 =$ _____

(d) $+28 / +7 =$ _____

(e) $-45 / -5 =$ _____

(f) $+54 / -9 =$ _____

(g) $+42 / +6 =$ _____

(h) $-56 / -7 =$ _____

(i) $+32 / -8 =$ _____

(j) $+63 / +9 =$ _____

(k) $-35 / -7 =$ _____

(l) $-81 / +9 =$ _____

(m) $-18 / +3 =$ _____

(n) $+35 / -5 =$ _____

(o) $-63 / +7 =$ _____

(p) $-32 / -4 =$ _____

(q) $+56 / -8 =$ _____

(r) $-42 / +7 =$ _____

(s) $-54 / -6 =$ _____

(t) $+45 / +9 =$ _____

(u) $-28 / +7 =$ _____

(v) $+64 / +4 =$ _____

(w) $-72 / -8 =$ _____

(x) $+36 / -3 =$ _____

(y) $+24 / -4 =$ _____

(z) $-22 / -2 =$ _____

(?) $+50 / +2 =$ _____

(@) $-25 / -5 =$ _____

(#) $+30 / -6 =$ _____

($) $-40 / +5 =$ _____

(%) $+60 / -5 =$ _____

(&) $-30 / +3 =$ _____

(*) $+16 / +4 =$ _____

(>) $-50 / -5 =$ _____

(<) $0 / -3 =$ _____

(=) $-24 / -6 =$ _____

SECOND, circle all letters or symbols marking problems with answers between or including 0 to 6 and -25 to -7 on the number line.

THIRD, shade these symbols or letters in the grid below.

```
@ d x u p f c b z h a w = p n r x h # L % p > i % & b # t d L o $ e i b @ m h * L @ % ? $ o x f
a e g t v n ? Y k m d ? j u b f @ i < ? u k g X s e p u Y h = ? s w C s # q i k f s n y b v s f
= z i * h $ w > x g l s g # o v = z $ f s # r ? a m z g s j @ m g > % h Y L ? < o t * w d @ < z
b v # & r o e i % P $ V < m * Y t e d Z < o v r h * v p f m n r u m & j g = J c = V > g = r ?
< > w q s L m u q V @ f = h c ? L P b j h t Y f w # c i w > a # Y V * ? u $ e a Y X Z j k e w ?
c k $ Y Y z @ d # Y r k u & z > q g w = @ p e < n k > ? u e b f j z m d k w > & # f $ u % q & c
```

FOURTH, unscramble the letters to reveal the name of the mystery athlete described above.

___ ___   ___ ___ ___ ___ ___   ___ ___ ___ ___ ___

Name _____

OLYMPIC MOMENTS, 1996

The 1996 Summer Olympics in Atlanta brought many memorable moments to sports fans around the world. Muhammed Ali's lighting of the flame at the Opening Ceremonies was one of the highlights for his many fans. For the United States, the thrill of watching the women's gymnastic team win gold was a highlight of the games. Although Shannon Miller ably captained the team, the most memorable gymnastic performance was on the vault by a tiny gymnast with a strained ankle. Solve the equations below to spell out the name of the athlete who had to be carried to the medal stand by her coach Bela Karolyi.

Solve these equations for x.

[1] $4 - x = 11$ _____

[2] $x - 12 = 4$ _____

[3] $3x = -18$ _____

[4] $54 = -9x$ _____

[5] $x + 9 = 1$ _____

[6] $5 - 3x = -31$ _____

[7] $-6x - 4 = -40$ _____

[8] $3 - 7x = 45$ _____

[9] $2(4 - x) = 14$ _____

[10] $-3(x + 5) = -45$ _____

Match the answer from each problem to a letter in the alphabet below. Then place that letter into the appropriate blank at the bottom of the page.

A	+8	J	+13	S	+12
B	−11	K	−7	T	+6
C	+3	L	−15	U	−3
D	+9	M	−12	V	+14
E	+16	N	+15	W	−16
F	+5	O	−10	X	+11
G	+10	P	+7	Y	+4
H	−4	Q	−13	Z	−5
I	−8	R	−6		

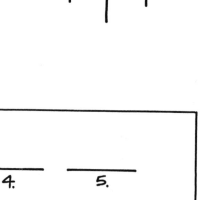

_____ 1.　_____ 2.　_____ 3.　_____ 4.　_____ 5.

_____ 6.　_____ 7.　_____ 8.　_____ 9.　_____ 10.

Name

MAKING THE GRADE

Bob is in a mess. If he doesn't pass the next math test, he will be ineligible to play basketball this semester. You have been assigned to tutor him. You'll need to practice solving equations with integers to see if you're ready to be his tutor.

1. $x + -2 = 7$

2. $y - (-3) = 4$

3. $-3x = 9$

4. $r + 23 = -19$

5. $x - 9 = 22$

6. $-5 + p = 19$

7. $-5x = 25$

8. $p - 13 = 21$

9. $s + -7 = -5$

10. $c - 3 = 0$

11. $-3 + 2x = 7$

12. $y + 2y - 5 = -26$

Bill is beginning to understand the problems above, but he has a very hard time with equations that have fractions in them. Write a detailed explanation of each of the problems below to assist him.

13. $-4y = +8$

_____

_____

14. $n + 30 = -14$

_____

_____

15. $m - 18 = -26$

_____

_____

16. $-5 t = -110$

_____

_____

17. Bill showed you his review sheet. You need to correct his work. Look over his solution and then make corrections to his problem.

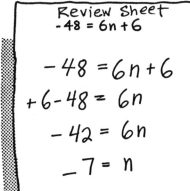

Review Sheet
$-48 = 6n + 6$

$-48 = 6n + 6$
$+6 - 48 = 6n$
$-42 = 6n$
$-7 = n$

Corrections
$-48 = 6n + 6$

Name

GOING FOR THE GOLD

At the Summer Olympics in Atlanta Dot Richardson captured the essence of the games by her winning smile and team spirit. Not only was she an Olympic athlete, but she was also resident physician at the USC School of Medicine. She called her autobiography *Living the Dream,* and she landed six endorsement contracts. Plot the following points to discover the sport at which she excelled in the Olympics.

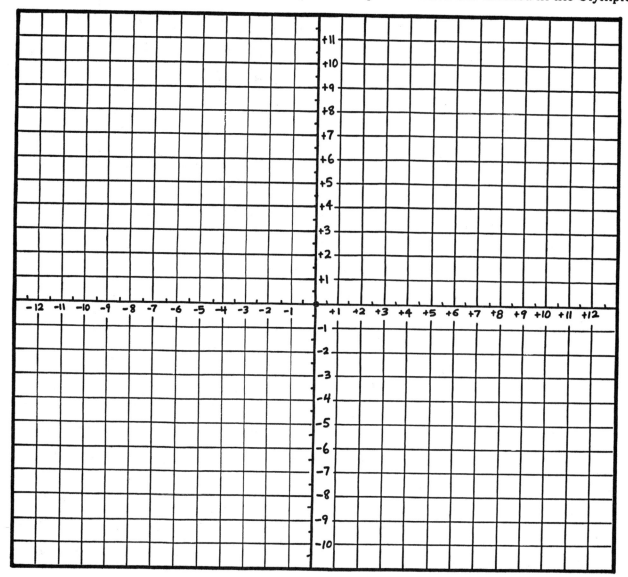

A. Plot these points and connect them in order.

(–2, –4)	(8, 2)	(12, –2)	(4, –10)
(0, –3)	(5, –1)	(10, –5)	(2, –8)
(1, –2)	(9, 2)	(11, –6)	(1, –7)
(2, –1)	(10, 1)	(11, –7)	(0, –6)
(3, 0)	(10.5, 0)	(10, –8)	(–1, –5)
(4, 2)	(8, –2)	(8, –8)	(–2, –4)
(7, 3)	(11, 0)	(6, –9)	

B. Plot these points and connect them in order.

(–2, 5)	(–11, 7)	(–2, 7)	(2, 9)
(–8, 1)	(–8, 10)	(–2, 5)	(1.5, 10.5)
(–9, 1)	(–6, 10.5)	(–1, 6)	(0, 10)
(–10, 3)	(–4, 9.5)	(0, 7)	(–2, 9)
(–11, 5)	(–3, 8.5)	(1, 8)	(–3, 8.5)

Name _____

APPENDIX

CONTENTS

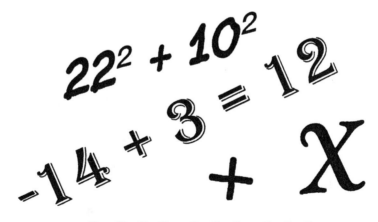

GLOSSARY OF MATH TERMS

ABSOLUTE VALUE—The distance a number is from 0 on the number line.

ADDEND—A number being added in an addition problem.
Ex: In the equation 4 + 7 = 11, 4 and 7 are addends.

ADDITION—An operation combining two or more numbers.

ADDITIVE INVERSE—For a given number, the number that can be added to give a sum of 0.
Ex: −4 is the additive inverse of + 4 because −4 + (+4) = 0.

ASSOCIATIVE PROPERTY FOR ADDITION AND MULTIPLICATION—Rule stating that the grouping of addends or factors does not affect the sum or product.
Ex: (3 + 6) + 9 = 3 + (6 + 9)
(2 x 4) x 7 = 2 x (4 x 7)

AVERAGE—The sum of a set of numbers divided by the number of addends.
Ex: The average of 1, 2, 7, 3, 8, and 9 =
$$\frac{1 + 2 + 7 + 3 + 8 + 9}{6} = 5$$

AXIS—A number line which may be vertical or horizontal.

COEFFICIENT—In the expression *8x*, 8 is the coefficient of *x*.

COMMON FACTOR—A whole number which is a factor of two or more numbers.
Ex: 3 is a factor common to 6, 9, and 12.

COMMON MULTIPLE—A whole number that is a multiple of two or more numbers.
Ex: 12 is a multiple common to 6 and 4.

COMMUTATIVE PROPERTY FOR ADDITION AND MULTIPLICATION—Rule stating that the order of addends or factors has no effect on the sum or product.
Ex: 3 + 9 = 9 + 3 and 4 x 7 = 7 x 4

COORDINATES—A pair of numbers which gives the location of a point on a plane.

COORDINATE PLANE—A grid on a plane with two perpendicular lines (axes).

DECIMAL SYSTEM—A numeration system based on grouping by tens.

DIFFERENCE—The answer in a subtraction problem.

DIGIT—A symbol used to write numerals. In the decimal system, there are ten digits: 0–9.

DISTRIBUTIVE PROPERTY FOR MULTIPLICATION OVER ADDITION—Rule stating that when the sum of two or more addends is multiplied by another number, each addend must be multiplied separately, and the products added together.
Ex: 3 x (4 + 6 + 9) = (3 x 4) + (3 x 6) + (3 x 9)

DIVIDEND—A number which is to be divided in a division problem.
Ex: In 2640 ÷ 40 = 66, the dividend is 2640.

DIVISIBILITY—A number is divisible by a given number if the quotient is a whole number.

DIVISION—The operation of finding a missing factor when the product and one factor are known.

DIVISOR—The factor used in a division problem for the purpose of finding the missing factor
Ex: In 2640 ÷ 40 = 66, the divisor is 40.

EQUATION—A mathematical sentence which states that two expressions are equal.
Ex: 7 x 9 = 3 + (4 x 15) is an equation.

ESTIMATE—An approximation or rough calculation.

EVEN NUMBER—One of the set of whole numbers having 2 as a factor.

EXPANDED NOTATION—Method of writing a numeral to show the value of each digit.
Ex: 5327 = 5000 + 300 + 20 + 7

EXPONENT—A numeral telling how many times a number is to be used as a factor.
Ex: In 6^3, the exponent is 3.
      6^3 means 6 x 6 x 6, or 216.

FACTOR—One of two or more numbers that can be multiplied to find a product.
Ex: In 6 x 9 = 54, 6 and 9 are factors.

GREATEST COMMON FACTOR—The largest number that is a factor of two other numbers.
Ex: 6 is the greatest common factor of 18 and 24

GRID—A set of horizontal and vertical lines spaced uniformly.

IDENTITY ELEMENT FOR ADDITION—Zero is the identity element for addition, because any number plus 0 = that number.
Ex: 3 + 0 = 3

IDENTITY ELEMENT FOR MULTIPLICATION—One is the identity element for multiplication, because any number multiplied by 1 equals that number.
Ex: 17 x 1 = 17

INEQUALITY—A number sentence showing that two groups of numerals stand for different numbers. The signs < and > and ≠ show inequality.
Ex: 7 + 5 ≠ 12 – 9

INTEGER—Any member of the set of positive or negative counting numbers and zero.
. . . –4, –3, –2, –1, 0, 1, 2, 3, 4, . . .

INVERSE—Opposite. Addition and subtraction are inverse operations. Multiplication is the inverse of division.

LEAST COMMON DENOMINATOR—The smallest whole number which is a multiple of the denominators of two or more fractions.
Ex: 12 is the least common denominator for ⅓ and ¾.

LEAST COMMON MULTIPLE—The smallest whole number which is divisible by each of two or more given numbers.
Ex: 18 is the least common multiple of 2, 6, 9, and 18.

MULTIPLE—The product of a whole number and any other whole number.
Ex: 12 is a multiple of 3 because 3 x 4 = 12.

MULTIPLICATION—An operation involving repeated addition.
Ex: 4 x 5 means 4 + 4 + 4 + 4 + 4.

MULTIPLICATIVE INVERSE—For any given number, the number that will yield a product of 1.
Ex: 4/3 is the multiplicative inverse of ¾ because 4/3 x ¾ = 1.

NAPIER'S BONES—A set of sticks or rods bearing multiplication facts.

NEGATIVE INTEGER—One of a set of counting numbers that is less than 0.

NUMBER—A mathematical idea concerning the amount contained in a set.

NUMBER LINE—A line which has numbers corresponding to points along it.

NUMERAL—A symbol used to represent or name a number.

NUMERATION SYSTEM—A system of symbols used to express numbers.

ODD NUMBER—A whole number belonging to the set of numbers equal to (n x 2) + 1.

OPEN SENTENCE—A number sentence with a variable.

OPPOSITE PROPERTY—A property that states if the sum of two numbers is zero, then each number is the opposite of the other.
Ex: −4 + 4 = 0, so −4 and 4 are opposites.

ORDERED PAIR—A pair of numbers in a certain order, the order being of significance.

ORDINAL NUMBER—A number telling the place of an item in an ordered set. *Sixth* describes an ordinal number.

ORIGIN—The beginning point on a number line. The origin is often zero.

PERIODS—Groups of three digits in numbers.

millions period —7 2 3, 3 0 1, 6 1 1— units period
thousands period

PLACE VALUE—The value assigned to a digit due to its position in a numeral.

POSITIVE INTEGER—One of a set of counting numbers that is greater than zero.

PRIME FACTOR—A factor that is a prime number; 1, 2, and 5 are prime factors of 20.

PRIME NUMBER—A number that has as its only whole number factors one and itself.
2, 3, 7, 11 . . . are prime numbers.

PROPERTY OF 0—A property which states that for any integer plus zero, the sum is that integer.

PROPERTY OF 1—A property which states that any number multiplied by 1 will equal the number.

PRODUCT—The answer in a multiplication problem.
Ex: In 66 x 40 = 2640, the product is 2640.

QUOTIENT—The answer in a division problem.
Ex: In 2640 ÷ 40 = 66, the quotient is 66.

REAL NUMBERS—Any number that is a positive number, a negative number, or zero.

REMAINDER—The number (less than the divisor) that is left when division is finished.

RENAME (or regroup)—To name numbers with a different set of numerals.

ROUNDING—Getting an approximate amount by dropping the digits after a given place.

SCIENTIFIC NOTATION—A method of expressing very large or very small numbers as a value between 1 and 10 multiplied by a power of 10.
Ex: 623,000 in scientific notation = 6.23×10^5; .00025 in scientific notation = 2.5×10^{-4}

SEQUENCE—A continuous series of numbers ordered according to a pattern.

SKIP COUNT—Counting by skipping a certain number of digits. (Counting by 2s, 5s, 10s, etc.)

SUBTRACTION—The operation of finding a missing addend when the sum and the other addends are known.

SUM—The answer in an addition problem resulting from the combination of two or more addends.

VARIABLE—A symbol in a number sentence which could be replaced by a number.
Ex: In 3 + 9x = 903, x is the variable.

WHOLE NUMBER—A member of the set of numbers 0, 1, 2, 3, 4, . . .

X-AXIS—The horizontal number line on a coordinate grid.

Y-AXIS—The vertical number line on a coordinate grid.

ZERO—The number of members in an empty set.

WHICH NUMBER IS WHICH?

Number: .... a mathematical idea concerning the amount contained in a set

Ordinal Number: .... a number telling the place of an item in an ordered set (e.g., sixth, ninth)

Even Numbers: .... numbers that are divisible by 2

Odd Numbers: .... numbers that are not even

Prime Number: .... a number whose only factors are 1 and itself

Composite Numbers: .... all numbers that are not prime

Whole Number: .... a member of the set of numbers (0, 1, 2, 3, 4, 5, 6, 7 . . .)

Fractional Number: .... a number that can be written in the form $\frac{a}{b}$ with a and b being any numbers, with the exception that b cannot be 0

Mixed Fractional Number: .... a number that has a whole number part and a fractional number part

Decimal Number: .... number written with a decimal point to express a fraction whose denominator is 10 or a multiple of 10

Mixed Decimal Number: .... a number that has a whole number part and a decimal number part

Integers: .... the set of whole numbers (. . . 4, –3, –2, –1, 0, 1, 2, 3, 4 . . .)

Positive Integers: .... the numbers to the right of 0 on a number line

Negative Integers: .... the numbers to the left of 0 on a number line

Rational Number: .... a number that can be written as a ratio $\frac{a}{b}$ where both a and b are integers and b is not 0 (all integers and decimals that terminate or repeat)

Irrational Number: .... a number that cannot be written as a quotient of two integers (decimals that neither repeat nor terminate)

Real Numbers: .... rational and irrational numbers together are the set of real numbers

Opposite Numbers: .... two numbers that are the same distance from 0 but are on opposite sides of 0 on a number line

Exponential Number: .... a number with an exponent (a number written next to and above the base number to show how many times the base is to be used as a factor)

Digit: .... one number in a numeral that holds a particular place

Basic Skills/Whole Numbers & Integers 6-8+

SOME PROMINENT PROPERTIES

Commutative Property for Addition: .... The order in which numbers are added does not affect the sum.

$$5 + 7 = 7 + 5$$

Commutative Property for Multiplication: .... The order in which numbers are multiplied does not affect the product.

$$9 \times 6 = 6 \times 9$$

Associative Property for Addition: .... The way in which numbers are grouped does not affect the sum.

$$5 + (2 + 7) = (5 + 2) + 7$$

Associative Property for Multiplication: .... The way in which numbers are grouped does not affect the product.

$$(5 \times 6) \times 3 = 5 \times (6 \times 3)$$

Distributive Property: .... To multiply a sum of numbers, you can add the numbers and then multiply the sum.

$$7 \times (5 + 3) = 7 \times 8 = 56$$

or,

you can multiply the numbers separately and then add the products.

$$7 \times (5 + 3) = (7 \times 5) + (7 \times 3) = 35 + 21 = 56$$

Identity Property for Addition: .... The sum of zero and any number is that number.

$$8 + 0 = 8 \quad 533 + 0 = 533$$

Identity Property for Multiplication: .... The product of 1 (one) and any number is that number.

$$8 \times 1 = 8 \quad 799 \times 1 = 799$$

Opposites Property: .... If the sum of two numbers is zero, then each number is the opposite of the other.

$$-7 \text{ is the opposite of } +7 \text{ because } -7 + (+7) = 0$$

Equation Properties: .... You can add or subtract the same number or multiply or divide by the same number on both sides of an equation and the result is still an equation.

$$x - 6 = 7$$
$$x - 6 + 6 = 7 + 6$$
$$x = 13$$

WHOLE NUMBERS & INTEGERS
SKILLS TEST

Questions 1–80 are each worth 1 point. Questions 81–90 are each worth 2 points. Total possible score: 100 pts.

1–3: Write these numerals in words.

1. 2,304,611 _____

   _____

2. 110,013 _____

   _____

3. 5,000,010 _____

   _____

4–6: Write the numerals represented by these words.

4. two hundred twenty-two thousand, seventeen

   _____

5. four million, seven hundred, ten

   _____

6. sixty-nine thousand, forty-three

   _____

7–11: Tell the value of the place that is underlined.

7. 605,319 _____

8. 2,000,000 _____

9. 153,966 _____

10. 2004 _____

11. 26,917,211 _____

12–16: Put the following numerals in order from smallest to largest. Write them on the lines.

600,006   661,106   601,160   666,601   610,116

12. _____

13. _____

14. _____

15. _____

16. _____

17–21: Put the following numerals in order from smallest to largest. Write them on the lines.

–17   21   –4   7   –6

17. _____

18. _____

19. _____

20. _____

21. _____

22. Which numbers below question 23 are PRIME numbers? _____

23. Which numbers below are COMPOSITE numbers? _____

20   7   3   6   19   8   23

24–29: Round these numbers according to directions.

24. 51,736 _____
    Round to the nearest hundred.

25. 9,374,196 _____
    Round to the nearest hundred.

26. 299, 566 _____
    Round to the nearest thousand.

27. 2,814,609 _____
    Round to the nearest thousand.

28. 874,331 _____
    Round to the nearest ten thousand.

29. 208,109 _____
    Round to the nearest ten thousand.

Name _____

30–34: Write the letter that shows the property represented by each equation.

A = Associative Property
C = Commutative Property
D = Distributive Property

_____ 30. $12 + 6 = 6 + 12$

_____ 31. $(4 + 3) + 8 = 4 + (3 + 8)$

_____ 32. $5(2 + 6) = 5 \times 2 + 5 \times 6$

_____ 33. $8(7 + 9) = 8 \times 16$

_____ 34. $20 \times 7 = 7 \times 20$

35. Which of these numbers are divisible by 3?

_____

8   39   16   31   57   18

36. Which of these numbers are NOT divisible by 6?

_____

9   18   21   22   15   30   24

37. Write the lowest common multiple of 9 and 18.

_____

38. Write the lowest common multiple of 4, 16, and 20. _____

39. What is the value of 100^3? _____

40. What is the value of 4^4? _____

41. What is the value of 6^3? _____

42. What is the value of 2×10^2? _____

43. What is the value of 3×10^3? _____

44. What is the value of $298{,}000 \div 10^2$? _____

45. What is the value of 5×10^4? _____

46. Give the opposite of –33. _____

47. Give the opposite of +16. _____

48–58: Solve these problems.

48. $21 + {-21} =$ _____

49. $-11 + 7 + -12 + 9 =$ _____

50. $-14 - -26 =$ _____

51. $-16 - -3 + -4 =$ _____

52. $5 \times -3 =$ _____

53. $-4 \times -7 =$ _____

54. $-18 \times 5 =$ _____

55. $-12 \div 4 =$ _____

56. $-72 \div -8 =$ _____

57. $-80 \div 10 =$ _____

58. $95 \div -5 =$ _____

59–65: Solve for n.

59. $-3 + -2 = n$ _____

60. $-4 \times -7 = n \times -4$ _____

61. $4(93 + 67) = n$ _____

62. $n + 88 = 199$ _____

63. $210 = 15n$ _____

64. $4n = 180$ _____

65. $n - 7116 = 861$ _____

66–70: Solve these.

66. $47 \times 10^2 =$ _____

67. $369 \times 111 =$ _____

68. $280 \div 20 =$ _____

69. $10^4 \times 20 =$ _____

70. $10^6 \div 10^2 =$ _____

71. $400{,}000 \div 100 =$ _____

72. $(600 + 739) - 400 =$ _____

73. $(-5 \times -5) + (-6 \times 3) =$ _____

74. $10^8 + 10 =$ _____

75. $2400 \div 600 =$ _____

Name _____

76–80: Solve for *y.*

76. $14 \times 10^4 = y$ _____

77. $y = 300,000 \div 10^3$ _____

78. $770y = -2310$ _____

79. $y(12 + -5) = -700$ _____

80. $(-3 + 15) - -10 = y$ _____

81–90: Solve these word problems. Each answer is worth 2 points.

_____ 81. Basketball Player Q earns $470,000 a year. Player B has a 3-year contract for $1,200,000 total. In three years, which player will earn more?

_____ How much more?

_____ 82. An arena for a diving championship holds 7000 people. It is at full capacity for 17 competitions. How many people attended in all 17 meets?

_____ 83. The temperature on the day of the ski race was –17° F at 6 A.M. in the morning. By 4 in the afternoon, it had risen 52° F. What was the temperature at 4 P.M.?

_____ 84. The high school booster club sold 1456 tickets to the Homecoming Game. This was twice as many as they had sold to the last game. How many did they sell for the last game?

_____ 85. Suzanne spent half her savings on new soccer shoes. After that, she bought a sweatsuit for $35 and new ski poles for $45. She had $10 left. How much did she spend on the soccer shoes?

_____ 86. Samantha and Sam jogged together every day for 5 weeks. Their total mileage was 140 miles each. If they each jogged the same distance each day, how far did each one jog each day?

_____ 87. The day of the outdoor skating competition, the temperature dropped 17° F before 8 A.M. It dropped another 22° F by noon. In the afternoon, the temperature increased 5° F by 2 P.M. If the temperature was –4° F at 2 P.M., what was it before 8 A.M.?

_____ 88. Wrestler Tom weighs 128 pounds, which is 37 pounds less than wrestler Jake, who weighs 14 pounds more than wrestler Bill. How much does Bill weigh?

_____ 89. Each member of a 16-person soccer team owns 7 pairs of soccer shoes. How many total shoes is that?

_____ 90. A basketball team scores 1485 points in a season. If 15 different players get equal playing time, what is the average number of points scored per player?

SCORE: Total Points _____ out of a possible 100 points

Name

WHOLE NUMBERS & INTEGERS
SKILLS TEST ANSWER KEY

Questions 1–80 are each worth 1 point. Questions 81–90 are each worth 2 points.

1. two million, three hundred four thousand, six hundred eleven
2. one hundred ten thousand, thirteen
3. five million, ten
4. 222,017
5. 4,000,710
6. 69,043
7. 6 hundred thousands
8. 0 ten thousands
9. 9 hundreds
10. 0 tens
11. 2 ten millions (or 20 millions)
12. 600,006
13. 601,160
14. 610,116
15. 661,106
16. 666,601
17. –17
18. –6
19. –4
20. 7
21. 21
22. 3, 7, 19, 23
23. 6, 8, 20
24. 51,700
25. 9,374,200
26. 300,000
27. 2,815,000
28. 870,000
29. 210,000

30. C
31. A
32. D
33. D
34. C
35. 39, 57, 18
36. 9, 21, 22, 15
37. 18
38. 80
39. 1,000,000
40. 256
41. 216
42. 200
43. 3000
44. 2980
45. 50,000
46. +33
47. –16
48. 0
49. –7
50. +12
51. –17
52. –15
53. +28
54. –90
55. –3
56. +9
57. –8
58. –19
59. –5
60. –7

61. 640
62. 111
63. 14
64. 45
65. 7977
66. 4700
67. 40,959
68. 14
69. 200,000
70. 10,000
71. 4000
72. 939
73. 7
74. 100,000,010
75. 4
76. 140,000
77. 300
78. –3
79. –100
80. +22
81. Q; $210,000
82. 119,000
83. 35° F
84. 728
85. $90
86. 2 miles
87. + 30°
88. 151 pounds
89. 224 shoes (112 pairs)
90. 99 points

ANSWERS

1. two million, seven hundred eighty-three thousand, seven hundred twenty-six
2. seven million, three hundred twenty-two thousand, five hundred sixty-four
3. one million, five hundred eighty-five thousand, five hundred eighty-seven
4. 2,833,511
5. 1,744,124
6. 3,711,043
7. 8,863,164
8. two million, three hundred eighty-two thousand, one hundred seventy-two
9. one million, eight hundred thirty-one thousand, one hundred twenty-two
10. four million, three hundred eighty-two thousand, two hundred ninety-seven
11. one million, six hundred seven thousand, one hundred eighty-three
12. 1,566,280
13. 372,242
14. 1,972,961

Page 11

1. $9,000,000
2. five million
3. ten millions
4. ten thousands
5. 400,000
6. $600
7. 100,000,000 (one hundred million)
8. 2
9. 100,000 (one hundred thousand)
10. 800,000 (eight hundred thousand)

Page 12

1. 3000 + 900 + 60 + 6
2. 1000 + 900 + 40 + 5
3. 700,000 + 60, 000 + 7,000 + 200
4. 100 + 60 + 2
5. 4000 + 900 + 60 + 2
6. 50,000 + 1,000 + 10 + 1
7. 2,000 + 900 + 60 + 2
8. 1,000 + 900 + 10 + 3
9. 200,000,000
10. 6,000 + 900 + 40 + 2
11. 3,000 + 600
12. 1,000 + 300 + 30 + 6

Page 13

1. NY Knicks—$1000
   LA Lakers—$600
   Chicago Bulls—$400
   Houston Rockets—$375
   LA Clippers—$275
   Charlotte Hornets—$180
   Minnesota Timberwolves—$174
2. 3 tickets to Chicago Bulls—$300
3. 5 tickets to Chicago Bulls—$800
4. 3 tickets to LA Clippers—$105
5. 5 tickets to Houston Rockets—$675
6. Minnesota, Charlotte, LA Clippers, Houston, Chicago
7. Answers will vary.

Page 14

1.	530	21.	3,000
2.	790	22.	3,000
3.	1,250	23.	5,000
4.	6870	24.	9,000
5.	800	25.	2,000
6.	40	26.	5,000
7.	10	27.	8,000
8.	60	28.	55,000
9.	570	29.	544,000
10.	2,270	30.	7,000
11.	600	31.	40,000
12.	1,200	32.	260,000
13.	600	33.	90,000
14.	800	34.	210,000
15.	1,100	35.	460,000
16.	400	36.	790,000
17.	600	37.	90,000
18.	4,000	38.	760,000
19.	4,200	39.	10,000
20.	900	40.	50,000

Page 15

A = 18	1. wildcats
B = 22	2. bengals
C = 27	
D = 12	3. lions
E = 23	4. panthers
G = 28	
H = 35	5. tigers
I = 60	
J = 33	6. bobcats
L = 29	7. cougars
N = 26	
O = 11	8. jaguars
P = 13	
R = 44	
S = 49	
T = 24	
U = 15	
W = 9	
Y = 17	

Pages 16–17

1. frame 1 = 9
   frame 2 = 16
2. a. frame 1 = 16
   b. frame 2 = 24
3. spare
   frame 1 = 19
   frame 2 = 28
4. a. 13
   b. 17
   c. 3
   d. 7
5. Scores in frames 1–2–3–4–5
   Brianna: 6–15–35–53–62
   Mark: 8–25–32–48–56
   Jana: 8–28–46–54–62
   Jay: 19–28–46–55–64

Page 18

1. a. 3
   b. 8
2. a. 7
   b. 7
3. a. C
   b. A
   c. C
   d. A
   e. C
   f. A
4. a. 7, 7
   b. 5
5. a. (12 + 7) +3   (May vary.)
   b. (6 x 8) x 2   (May vary.)
   c. 9 + (5 + 11)   (May vary.)
   d. (10 x 4) + (10 x 3)
   e. 6(5 + 2)
   f. (1 + 9) + 5   (May vary.)
   g. (7 x 4) x 12   (May vary.)
   h. 11 x (2 x 7)   (May vary.)
   i. 8 x (10 x 2)   (May vary.)
   j. 14 + (3 + 8)   (May vary.)

Page 19

1.	a. 0	c. 0	e. 4
	b. 2	d. ⅙	f. 9

2. a. inverse   d. identity   g. zero
   b. zero   e. identity   h. identity
   c. identity   f. inverse   i. identity

3.	1. E	4. B	7. A
	2. C	5. F	8. A
	3. D	6. E	

Page 20

1. 3, 6, 9, 12, 15, 18, 21, 24, 27, 30
2. 6, 12, 18, 24, 30, 36, 42, 48, 54, 60
3. 7, 14, 21, 28, 35, 42, 49, 56, 63, 70
4. 2, 4, 6, 8, 10, 12, 14, 16, 18, 20
5. a. Cougars 36; Panthers 34
   b. Bobcats 94; Wildcats 90
   c. Lions 36; Tigers 37
   d. Cougars 110; Jaguars 97

Page 21

1. 42–42	13. 45
2. 24 baseballs	14. 300
3. 60 pounds	15. 30
4. yes	16. 252
5–10. Answers will vary.	17. 60
11. 154	18. 624
12. 60	19. 750

Answers

Pages 22–23

1. I. 14 mi
   II. 15 mi
   III. 12 mi

2. I. 98 min
   II. 105 min
   III. 84 min

3. I. 20 mi
   II. 18 mi
   III. 19 mi

4. I. 120 min
   II. 108 min
   III. 114 min

5. I. A-B-E-H-L-O-S
   II. 21 mi

6. 105 min

7. 20 mi

Page 24

1. 5-$10
   3-$27
   7-$28   Total = $205
   4-$92
   8-$48

2. 9-$108
   6-$174
   7-$35   Total = $446
   27-$108
   3-$21

3. 5-$15
   3-$42
   7-$42   Total = $233
   2-$116
   9-$18

Page 25

1. $25 million
2. $8 million
3. $16 million
4. $7,142,857
5. $35 million
6. $15 million
7. $10 million
8. $400,000
9. a. $250,000
   b. $10,000

Page 26

C = 90		R = 632	
T = 700		P = 774	
O = 3		U = 29	
N = 8		L = 12	
A = 4		B = 31	
Y = 9		E = 22	
H = 6			

Answer: Coach Paul "Bear" Bryant

Page 27

1. yes   2. no   3. yes   4. yes   5. yes

	58	153	228	523	80	104	180	89	532	90
2	x		x		x	x	x		x	x
3		x	x				x			x
4			x		x	x	x		x	
5					x		x			x
6			x				x			x
10					x		x			x

Page 28

Answer reads: GO TEAM

Page 29

1. D
2. A
3. G
4. B
5. H
6. J
7. C
8. E
9. F
10. I
11. 392
12. 43,200
13. 1,000,000
14. 1,080,000
15. 576
16. 1,250,000
17. 196
18. 25
19. 2916
20. 1440
21. 5000
22. 1600

Page 30

1. 2 x 10² m; 4 x 10² m
2. 5 x 10² ft; 6 x 10³ in
3. 1 x 10⁵ mm
4. 60 m or 60,000 mm
5. 2390 mm or 890 cm
6. 8 x 10³ sec
7. 5 x 10⁴ yd
8. a. 1.2 x 10² sec   b. 2.3 10³ yd
9. 9 x 10³ mm
10. 95,000 mm

Page 31

1. 920 yds
2. 680 yds
3. 890 yds
4. 730 yds
5. 9500 yds
6. 1400 yds
7. 2700 yds
8. 3100 yds
9. 8700 yds
10. 10,600 yds
11. C-S-G-V-R-D-C or C-D-R-V-G-S-C
12. 23,870 yds

Page 32

1. 298 kph
2. 97 kph
3. 3529.56 kph
4. 206 kph
5. 556 kph
6. 45 kph
7. 230 kph
8. 1224 kph
9. 86 kph
10. 4 = parachutist
7 = racing pigeon
1 = jet plane
6 = water skier
3 = hydroplane
9 = board sailor
5 = ice yacht
2 = jet vehicle
8 = skateboarder

Page 33

1. 10,000
2. Answers will vary according to the year.
3. about 22 mph
4. $430
5. $145
6. $225
7. $390; $130 each installment
8. $200

Pages 34–35

1. $5
2. $9
3. Total: $261; each boy's share: $87
4. Mountain Biking $12; Picnic $14; Water Slide $18; Jet Ski $100; Video Games $9; Dinner $25; Bowling $27; Movies $5; Total $210. Each boy's share: $70
5. Total $104; Change $16
6. Total $42; $21 each
7. Total: $54; $18 each
8. $8
9. Total 18 hours or 6 hours per boy.
10. (a) 648; (b) approx. 23 cents

Pages 36–37

Estimates will vary somewhat.
1. $210
2. Answers will vary.
3. about $420–$450
4. a shadow cap
5. turf shirt: $30; pro jersey: $200; shadow cap: $20; Shipping $10 Total about $250
6. $750–$760
7. Answers will vary.
8. $170
9. $180–$190

Page 38

1. C = 8
2. S = 15
3. F = 12
4. G = 22
5. E = 7
6. T = 13
7. D = 19
8. P = 5

Page 39

1. M + 3 = 7 or M = 7 –3
2. 4P = 24 or P = $^{24}/_4$
3. L + 24 = 60 or L= 60 – 24
4. a. 4D = 48 or D = $^{48}/_4$
   b. 2D = W
5. 75B = 300 or B = $^{300}/_{75}$
6. 2H – 100 = 300
7. 2K = 6 or K = $^6/_2$
8. R + 11 = 15 or R = 15 – 11

Page 40

1. subtract
2. add
3. divided the number of points by the number of games
4. 873
5. Neither would win; it would be a 49–49 tie
6. M Jordan; 127
7. D Robinson; 78
8. M Jordan; 385
9. add
10. Answers will vary.

Page 41

1. A—Kerri Strug
2. F—Joe Montana
3. H—Juwan Howard
4. D—Penny Hardaway
5. E—Cigar
6. B—Evander Holyfield
7. G—Emmit Smith
8. C—Shaquille O'Neal

Pages 42–43

You will need to look at students' papers to see if points are located correctly on the number lines.

Page 44

St. Louis – Los Angeles – Antwerp

A =	+1	O =	–17
B =	+9	P =	–3
C =	–15	Q =	+12
D =	+3	R =	–14
E =	–8	S =	+6
F =	+14	T =	–21
G =	–6	U =	+7
H =	–16	V =	–18
I =	–5	W =	+15
J =	–4	X =	–13
K =	–12	Y =	+13
L =	+5	Z =	+18
M =	–17	Blank =	–11
N =	+16		

Page 45

Name: Coubertin
Motto: Faster, Higher, Stronger

1. –49	11. –42	21. –56
2. –36	12. +72	22. +72
3. +65	13. +48	23. +48
4. +36	14. –72	24. –56
5. –72	15. –56	25. –36
6. –56	16. +42	26. +20
7. +48	17. –54	27. 0
8. –54	18. 0	28. –72
9. +20	19. +42	29. –56
10. +81	20. –72	

Page 46

1. 63
2. 63
3. –63
4. –63
5. 21
6. –21
7. –21
8. 21
9. 22
10. –22
11. –22
12. 22
13. 180
14. –180
15. 180
16. –180
17. 660
18. –660
19. –660
20. 660
21. 24, 18, 12, 6, 0, –6, –12, –18, –24
22. –60, –42, –24, –6, 12, 30, 48, 66, 84
23. –35, –25, –15, –5, 5, 15, 25, 35, 45
24. +
25. +
26. –
27. 64
28. –490
29. 0
30. –11, 700

Page 47

a.	+6	m.	–6	y.	–6
b.	0	n.	–7	z.	+11
c.	–8	o.	–9	?.	+25
d.	+4	p.	+8	@.	+5
e.	+9	q.	–7	#.	–5
f.	–6	r.	–6	$.	–8
g.	+7	s.	+9	%.	–12
h.	+8	t.	+5	&.	–10
i.	–4	u.	–4	*.	+4
j.	+7	v.	+16	>.	+10
k.	+5	w.	+9	<.	0
l.	–9	x.	–12	=.	+4

Answer: Tiger Woods

Page 48

1. –7
2. +16
3. –6
4. –6
5. –8
6. +12
7. +6
8. –6
9. –3
10. +10

Answer: Kerri Strug

Page 49

1. x = 9
2. y = 1
3. x = –3
4. r = –42
5. x = 31
6. p = 24
7. x = –5
8. p = 34
9. s = 2
10. c = 3
11. x = 5
12. y = –7
13–16. Explanations will vary.
17.   –48 = 6n + 6
     –6 – 48 = 6n
     –54 = 6n
     –9 = n

Page 50